THE
ANATOMY
OF
DIRTY
WORDS

*Man lives in a symbolic universe.
Language, myth, art and religion
are parts of this universe. They are
the varied threads which weave the
symbolic net, the tangled web of
human experience.*

*No longer can man confront real-
ity immediately; he cannot see it,
as it were, face to face. Physical
reality seems to recede in propor-
tion as man's symbolic activity ad-
vances. Instead of dealing with the
things themselves man is in a sense
constantly conversing with himself.
He has so enveloped himself in
linguistic forms, in artistic images,
in mythical symbols or religious
rites that he cannot see or know
anything except by the interposi-
tion of this artificial medium. His
situation is the same in the theo-
retical as in the practical sphere.
Even here man does not live in a
world of hard facts, or according
to his immediate needs and desires.
He lives rather in the midst of
imaginary emotions, in hopes and
fears, in illusions and disillusions,
in his fantasies and dreams. "What
disturbs and alarms man," said
Epictetus, "are not the things, but
his opinions and fancies about the
things."*

ERNST CASSIRER: *An Essay on Man*

# THE
ANATOMY OF
DIRTY
WORDS

by

EDWARD SAGARIN

with an Introduction by
PROFESSOR ALLEN WALKER READ
Columbia University

LYLE STUART, PUBLISHER
1962

TO MY SON FRED —

May you never be at a loss for words

TABLE OF CONTENTS

Introduction, *by Allen Walker Read*   9

Acknowledgments   13

1. *Taboos Without Totems*   17

2. *The Handwriting on the Wall*   43

3. *The Policy of the Big Stick*   79

4. *Sticks and Stones Will Break My Bones*   105

5. *Euphemist, What's the Good Word?*   113

6. *Luv Is a Three-Letter Word*   121

7. *Linguistics: Erotica and Curiosa*   145

8. *In the Beginning There Was a Seed*   153

9. *To the Victors Belong the Soiled*   159

Footnotes, Elaborations, and Explanations   175

Bibliography and References   187

General Index   203

Index of Words and Phrases   209

INTRODUCTION

by *Allen Walker Read*

THE PART that words play in determining attitude is an important subject that merits continual probing. The so-called "dirty words" make a special problem. What is the reason for the strong emotional impact that they so often have? Our society has developed what may be called, I think, "word fetishism." Just as fetishes of many kind are the source of neurotic behavior, so word fetishes cause unhealthy emotional responses. Obscenity emerges out of unhealthy attitudes towards sex and the bodily functions. Not only are "dirty words" a symptom of those attitudes, but they serve to perpetuate the attitudes.

In this book Edward Sagarin points out the ironies and paradoxes in the socio-linguistic matrix where this interaction of words and attitudes takes place. It is especially curious that "respectable" members of society, when they inculcate and enforce the word taboos, are ensuring that the unhealthy attitudes will continue. Our moralists and "guardians of society" feel that the sex drive is so disordering that it must be hedged about by interdicts and prohibitions. This results in a general fear of any rich, fulfilling practice of sex. In the antisexual atmosphere thus created, "right-minded" people actually prefer, perhaps without realizing it, to have a layer of word fetishes that will divert sex interests from wholesome outlets into a verbal welter of disgusting utterances. The great tragedy of our society is the general failure to achieve warm, outgoing love as the normal relationship between individuals, and the very language itself all too often seems to "do dirt" on love.

The most outstanding defense of continuing the dirtiness of words has come, oddly enough, from the pen of a sensitive, thoughtful woman novelist, Katherine Anne Porter. As she wrote:

> My contention is that obscenity is real, is necessary as expression, a safety valve against the almost intolerable pressures and strains of relationship between men and women, and not only between men and women but between any human being and his unmanageable world.

If we distort, warp, abuse this language which is the seamy side of the noble language of religion and love, indeed the necessary defensive expression of insult towards the sexual partner and contempt and even hatred of the insoluble stubborn mystery of sex itself which causes us such fleeting joy and such cureless suffering, what have we left for a way of expressing the luxury of obscenity which, for an enormous majority of men, by their own testimony, is half the pleasure of the sexual act? [*Encounter,* XII, No. 2 (February, 1960), 72.]

I refuse to accept the situation that she postulates. Anyone who believes in a "necessary defensive expression of insult towards the sexual partner" needs to have his sex attitudes revised and reformed. It is not a simple matter to make such reorientations, and so explosive is the sex power that it may take many generations. But an enlightened individual cannot acquiesce in this aspect of our culture. If Miss Porter lived among headhunters, she ought to be against headhunting. She shows, I think, that she has been victimized by our cultural attitudes. Does "half the pleasure of the sexual act" really lie in "the luxury of obscenity"? She attributes this attitude to "an enormous majority of men" and seems to accept it without turning a hair. If her observation is true, she is describing an unwholesome situation, and she ought not to acquiesce in it so complacently. She needs Mr. Sagarin's book badly, and I hope she will take it to heart.

In a study of my own over twenty-five years ago, I tackled this problem and still subscribe to what I wrote at that time:

I believe that for the perfectly civilized person,

obscenity simply would not exist. He would have pleasurable sex stimulation, truly enough, and it would often be delicate and insinuating; but the stimulation would not carry with it the intent to degrade and to soil sex. When self-discipline must be applied because of circumstance or because of regard for his welfare, he would not take refuge in arbitrary fetishes but would face his problems with clear-eyed, intelligent determination. He would regard only with pity those who take a sly, lip-licking pleasure in obscenity. Being normal in the world today consists in having the neuroses that most other people have. A truer, more realistic adjustment is worth trying for. [*Lexical Evidence from Folk Epigraphy in Western North America* (Paris, 1935), p. 16.]

The present book puts the following issue clearly before us: can our society achieve wholesome, enlightened attitudes toward the physical functions? There is no simple answer, when an increased use of the "dirty words" would, as Edward Sagarin so well points out, merely serve to reinforce the undesirable attitudes. At present our pattern of usage has blockages and barriers built into it. By giving the matter thoughtful consideration, by approaching it with frank, open-minded discussion, we can reduce the obsessive element and, little by little, bring about an amelioration in society as a whole.

ACKNOWLEDGMENTS

AN AUTHOR has many debts, and he is fortunate if, after acknowledging the aid he has received from others, he can feel that a part of his work is his own.

The conceptualization contained in this book came to me during the course of studies of the relationship of language and culture, and particularly during my studies of the work of Edward Sapir and Benjamin Whorf. My first and greatest debt, then, is to these authors, as well as to several members of the staff of Brooklyn College, who first introduced me to the Sapir-Whorf hypothesis.

A great deal of the literature search and the bibliographical work that went into this book was done at the library of the Institute for Sex Research (founded by the late Dr. Alfred C. Kinsey), located on the campus of Indiana University, in Bloomington. I am deeply grateful to the directors of the Institute and their librarians, without whose cooperation a serious study of this subject would be well-nigh impossible.

I should like to express my appreciation to Dr. Albert Ellis, psychotherapist and author, who has had such a deep influence on my own thinking, and who gave this manuscript his critical reading.

I wish to acknowledge the aid of several faculty members at Brooklyn College, who read this manuscript in whole or in part, and gave me the benefit of their criticisms and suggestions. These include Dr. Rex Hopper, chairman of the Department of Sociology and Anthropology; Mr. Gerald Platt, visiting instructor of sociology during the summer of 1960; and several others. The kind and valuable assistance of these and other staff members at Brooklyn College is appreciated; it is hardly necessary to add that they are in no way responsible for what I have written in this book.

With deep gratitude, I wish to acknowledge my debt to Professor Allen Walker Read, who has so kindly written the foreword to this work, and who read an earlier version and made many valuable suggestions. Although I did not gain access to certain of Mr. Read's work on this subject until after I had completed the earlier version of this book, I found that he had expressed a viewpoint strikingly similar to my own, predating my work by about twenty-five years.

In fact, on several occasions during the preparation of this manuscript, I discovered that someone had written a work which, in certain respects, was remarkably similar to what I had just finished putting down on paper. The entire theme of this book was expressed by Dr. Albert Ellis in an "impolite interview" (cited in the bibliography), which I saw for the first time when I handed Dr. Ellis the first draft of what was then still a little essay. That I found my ideas running parallel to his could only please me, for he represents one of the few voices of sanity in a sad and bewildering world.

A second instance of independent arrival at similar material struck me when I gained access to the work of Mr. Read, who had not only made observations many years ago close to those I am making herein, but in one instance the two of us had, independently (except that his work came long before mine) coined the same word to fill what we felt was a gap in the language. Not only the concept of cacophemism, but the very word, with a spelling identical to that which I propose, is found in a work of his (likewise acknowledged in the bibliography).

When something like this happens, there is first a feeling of frustration; try as one might to be original, someone had come along and said the same thing, and probably said it better, before you were there. But this is just a passing moment, soon replaced by the gratification upon seeing a clear expression of ideas so congruent with one's own.

Nevertheless, what I have sought to do in this work is

to take the observations of Ellis, Read, and others one step further, by integrating them into the Sapir-Whorf hypothesis, and accumulating evidence to indicate that the manner in which modern man utilizes obscenities is not only a reflection of the antibiological bias of this culture, but then reinforces this very bias. The circle is vicious and self-perpetuating.

Finally, I am indebted to many people who, wittingly or otherwise, made contributions to this book. Some searched for and suggested expressions, lest I might overlook them; others used expressions in my presence, or even spoke on the streets, in subways, or restaurants in tones loud enough for me to overhear. A field study is sometimes a lesson in eavesdropping.

No doubt, despite the literature I have perused and the field work I have pursued, some expressions of importance, that fit into my theme, or others that may challenge it, have been overlooked. I shall welcome such information from my readers, and shall try to keep this compendium up-to-date.

Edward Sagarin

1 *Taboos Without Totems*

ONE

TUDENTS of the social scene have for many years recognized that the structure of language is a powerful tool for an understanding of a culture.

Some languages, it would appear, have a fuller vocabulary than others; an abundance of words to denote that which is described, in another tongue, with just a single word. An investigation of such a situation reveals, not an accident, but a reflection of how a society is organized.

There are seeming gaps in some languages, words that might be said, by cross-linguistic comparison, to be missing. Yet, those for whom this is the native tongue, and particularly the sole one, could hardly be aware of a deficiency. Other people, coming from a different society, would find it quite bewildering to understand how a thought and concept, so natural and vital to them, might have no means of being communicated. They would literally be at a loss for words.

Not only the vocabulary, but the sentence structure, the syntax and grammar, even the intonations and hesitations, are more than accidents in the evolutionary development of a language. As an example, in some languages sentences are constructed around the words of doing, which we call verbs, an indication of the superior position that the concept of action, as contrasted with objects, holds in the societies where this manner of speech prevails.

One of the pioneers in the study of the relationship of culture to language, Edward Sapir, wrote:

> That language is a perfect symbolism of experience, that in the actual context of behavior it cannot be divorced from action, and that it is the carrier of an infinitely nuanced expressiveness are universally valid psychological facts.[1]

For Sapir, however, language not only reflected a culture and hence permitted one the better to understand it; language influenced and conditioned behavior as well. "Language is a cultural or social product and must be understood as such," Sapir wrote,[2] proceeding further to point out that it powerfully conditions all our thinking about social problems and processes. Human beings do not live in the objective world alone, not alone in the world of social activity as ordinarily understood, but are very much at the mercy of the particular language which has become the medium of expression for their society.[3]

Thus, language is both a reflection of how we look at the world and at the same time determines how we shall look at the world. The universe around us is there for each of us to see, but different individuals and peoples will see this universe in divergent ways. Not only will this determine the development of the language, but the latter will itself determine how peoples look at the world; that is to say, how they structure reality in their own minds.

Another pioneer in linguistic analysis, B. L. Whorf, has described this process:

> We cut nature up, organize it into concepts, and ascribe significance as we do, largely because we are parties to an agreement to organize it in this way—an agreement that holds throughout our speech community and is codified in the patterns of our language. The agreement is, of course, an implicit and unstated one, *but its terms are absolutely obligatory.*[4]

Missionaries devoted to the task of bringing their messages to far-off lands have particularly been handicapped by the lack of equivalencies in the native tongue for words and concepts that required expression. The story of the virgin birth is sufficiently mystifying to Western man, but consider the bewilderment of communicating such an event—whether it be presented as historical, mythological, or symbolic—to a people whose vocabulary does not include the word *virgin,* and who have no need for such a word because children are universally inducted into sexual practices long before they have reached the age of puberty.[5]

In the cold climate of the far North, Eskimos live and find language very adequate for communication, although they do not have a word than can be considered the equivalent of the English *sin.*[6] It is a small linguistic lacuna, but it tells us more about Eskimo culture than one can find in many a popular article by a hurried traveler.

It was precisely a linguistic experience of this type that Sapir foresaw when he wrote that some day

> the attempt to master a primitive culture without the help of the language of its society will seem as amateurish as the labors of a historian who cannot handle the original documents of the civilization which he is describing.[7]

One is particularly struck by words, their abundance and their gaps, when one is concerned with the manner in which they hold the key to an understanding of kinship relations among various peoples.

In English, and in most of the other languages of the Western world, a single word describes my relationship to my mother's brother and to my father's brother. But in societies in which a sharp line of distinction is drawn between these two men, their closeness to me, their rights over me, and the mutual duties between myself and them, the single word would prove inadequate.

It would, indeed, be as inadequate as if there were only one word in English for mother and aunt. This is a situation which, in our society, seems absurdly incredible. However, one need but travel among numerous preliterate peoples, to find that no linguistic distinction is made between the biological mother and her sisters, or that a great distinction is made between a paternal uncle and a maternal one.

Where might lie the significance of a society's expressing through a single word what to Westerners are such distinct and different relationships as that of mother and aunt? What key does the language hold to an understanding of the society? The eminent anthropologist, A. R. Radcliffe-Brown, describes this singular terminology

> as a method of expressing and emphasizing the unity and solidarity of the patrilineal lineage group. A man belongs to a patrilineal lineage. He is closely connected with his mother's lineage, which plays an important part in his life, second only to that of his own. His connection with that lineage, being through his own mother, is with the first ascending generation. By the terminology, he treats all the members of that group, through three (or more) generations, beginning with that of his mother, as belonging to a single category; the females are "mothers" to him and the males are "mother's brothers." For all these persons, and for the group as a whole, he is a "sister's son." [8]

An aspect of language that has been investigated in a limited manner as a guide to an understanding of a culture is the use of proscribed or forbidden sounds, words, and phrases, not only in a contextual relationship, but as separate entities.

There are many thoughts that may not be verbalized for reasons other than linguistic. The defender of the right of free speech does not contend that under all conditions should a society allow an individual to say whatever he pleases, and suffer no punishments or sanctions as a consequence of his verbal acts.

For example, one may not lie under oath; one may not misrepresent orally what one is selling; one may not shout "Fire" in a crowded movie: these are but a few of numerous conditions when one is forbidden from uttering various sounds and words.

However, in these instances, the individual words are not tabooed. What is prohibited is their utterance in combination with other words, in a given context, to convey a thought or to incite an action which is condemned by society.

It would seem, on the face of it, that a word-sound by itself, separated from all that it might connote and denote, would not be forbidden. It would not be expected that a society might look upon a word, in and of itself, as evil, and order its members to refrain from pronouncing it.

Nevertheless, such sounds may indeed have been prohibited, or at least strongly proscribed, in many early societies. There seems to be some indication that a category, corresponding somewhat to our own English-language obscenities, has a counterpart among many preliterate peoples, and in many societies not at all Western in character. But whether the people uttering the words at times, suppressing them at others, regarded the words as obscene, or whether this quality was imputed to them by European and other travelers who took with them a set of European moral judgments, is today difficult to determine.

Thus the Reverend Duncan MacKenzie writes of obscene language at a death wailing in a primitive and ritual-bound group,[9] while Hanneken, in a description of the antiquity of classic Rome, describes obscenities at wedding ceremonies.[10] Junod tells of obscenities in rain-making rites in an African tribe,[11] Leem tells that obscenities were used by the Lapps while shooting,[12] and Macdonell gives an account of the rituals of family life in early India when the Vedic religion was dominant, in which he describes the sacrifice of a horse as an offering to the gods:

> The chief consort of the king lay down beside the dead horse, while obscene conversations were carried on between the priest and the women of the royal household.[13]

That obscenities corresponded at least among some groups to the terms considered obscene by modern Western man is seen from the example of Walter Roth, who is quoted by Read as reporting that among the Queensland aborigines, there is one quite acceptable word for vulva, and another that is one of the "most blackguardly words to use." [14]

A penetrating study of tabooed language among primitive peoples was made by the distinguished anthropologist, E. E. Evans-Pritchard.[15] He found proscribed language used on certain ceremonial occasions by many African peoples, but its use was collective, not individual. Words prohibited under ordinary circumstances became prescribed under others, particularly during religious ceremonies or joint economic undertakings, and Evans-Pritchard suggests functional values in obscenity that might have parallels in modern life.

For example, the withdrawal by society of its normal prohibitions might give special emphasis to the social value of an activity; the use of obscenity might canalize human emotion into prescribed and socially desirable channels at times of crises; and it might offer stimulus and reward to workers during a joint activity.

TWO

HE TABOOED word was not unknown in folk societies, nor among those groups of people living under what has variously been termed primitive, preliterate or unsophisticated conditions. It was usually a word that was not completely banned from the language, but one that was utterable under certain special conditions, in given circumstances or by particular persons.

Frequently, among such groups, there were proper names

that could not be spoken. In almost all societies, people are known by individual names, the word or sound formation by which they are called throughout their lives. But among some preliterate groups, no sooner does a man marry than he can no longer say the name of his wife's mother, a taboo that may follow him throughout his life.

A Caffre man, wrote Sir James Frazer in his now classic *The Golden Bough,* "may not mention the name of his mother-in-law." [16] The restriction is mutual: she may not pronounce the name of his mother. But his wife is even more severely restricted, for she

> is forbidden to pronounce even mentally the names of her father-in-law and of all her husband's male relatives in the ascending line; and whenever the emphatic syllable of any of their names occurs in another word, she must avoid it by substituting either another term or another syllable in its place. [17]

The taboo is not quite so great for her husband, for he is free "to utter words in which the emphatic syllable of her name (that is, his mother-in-law's) occurs." [18]

How absurd were these primitive people, to prohibit someone from pronouncing a word *even mentally*! How absurd, and how similar to some contemporary societies, where children are told that they must not *even think* dirty words!

Among many groups, the names of the dead may not be spoken, and people whose names are exactly the same as those of the departed thereupon change their name, because the similarity will attract the ghost of the dead. Thus, animism is not only reflected in the language, it is reinforced by the language and perpetuated by it.

Difficulties arise, because the members of the tribe are often named after objects, as in Western society a girl might be Rose or Daisy. The death of a person bearing such a name requires that the word for the object be dropped from the language, at least temporarily.

In the Judeo-Christian tradition, the concept of forbidding the name of the deity to be uttered was more limited than similar proscriptions governing names of gods or worldly rulers in other societies. In Burma, China, Korea, Cambodia, Zululand, New Zealand, and Tahiti, among other places on earth, Frazer points out, names of kings and emperors were hidden, held sacred, forbidden to be spoken, banished from the language, and if other words in the language even resembled that of the reigning monarch, the language itself had to be changed.[19]

"In England," the linguistic authority Bloomfield pointed out, "various terms of religion, such as *God, devil, heaven, hell, Christ, Jesus, damn,* are proper only in serious speech . . . (whereas) the male Cree Indian, for example, does not speak the names of his sisters and of some other female relatives; he explains the avoidance by saying, 'I respect her too much.' "[20]

Thus, when Moses went to Mount Sinai and received the Ten Commandments, a taboo was formulated not unlike that of other groups where fears of the supernatural were paramount. After the Lord Jehovah declared Himself to be "the Lord thy God," He forbade worship of any other gods, and called upon the Hebrews to work out a system of verbal taboos without objective totems. The latter, in fact, were specifically proscribed:

> Thou shalt not make unto thee any graven image, or any likeness of any thing that is in heaven above, or that is in the earth beneath, or that is in the water under the earth.[21]

And codified into the law of the Hebrews was a commandment destined to have a wide influence on the development of English-language profanity:

> Thou shalt not take the name of the Lord thy God in vain; for the Lord will not hold him guiltless that taketh His name in vain.[22]

ROM THE superstitious fears of unso
phisticated man to the ritualistic proscriptions of the self
proclaimed sophisticate, one discovers names, words, and
sounds that may not be spoken. But whatever may have been
the transgressions of his preliterate ancestors or his primitive
contemporaries against these rules, modern man, at least in
the midyears of the twentieth century, violates them with full,
abandon.

So frequent are these violations that one encounters not only the protests against the taboos, but likewise the reaction to the swing of the pendulum; the outbursts of those who see the taboos as hypocritical, and those who see in their violations a new prudery of men and women who are pretending to face the facts of nature.[23]

Unprintable, the words are today printed in books, dictionaries, and occasionally in magazines, although not in newspapers, whereas once they adorned only toilet walls and outlawed hard-core pornography. Yet, typical of a phenomenon in a state of flux, the words are often omitted from scientific and historical discussions of folklore, ethnography, linguistics, and even from discussions of obscenity.

Unutterable, the words can now be said, not only in the Army and Navy, among workers on the street, but even in polite and mixed company, although not in a college classroom, or over the radio, or on television.

Tabooed words are today known as *obscene language, dirty words, four-letter words,* and by a variety of other names, some misleading, some complimentary. They have by and large ceased to be part of the superstitions of society; they are rather a part of the shadow language of slang or argot, that ranges from the somewhat ungrammatical to the completely improper, from the colloquially quaint to the pejoratively dirty.

However, it is the belief of some that the frequency of use, the aura of quasi-respectability surrounding these words, is a sign of the degeneration of the times, of a growing immorality, of the decadence of a civilization in disintegration.

For those who view obscenity in this fashion, moral values seem to be dead in the modern world.

Others, however, see in the wide acceptance of obscene words among all classes of the population, all age groups and both sexes, a sign of man's liberation from outmoded and outlandish puritanism. They believe that sex, in the open, will flourish as a healthy manifestation of mankind.

Both groups, it is my sad conviction, are equally wrong, precisely because they have not understood that language reflects and reinforces a vision of reality; in this instance the reality as envisaged and as fixed in the language is one, as I shall demonstrate, of a mid-Victorian puritanism all the more nefarious because it is masquerading under the guise of hedonistic abandon.

FOUR

LANG in its origin may possibly be traced to educational and class differences in a community. In a completely folk and classless society, it is difficult to imagine that the speech of one individual may be more acceptable to the group as a whole than that of another.[24] With identical educational opportunities of all persons, there will be similar training in the use of language.

Later, as the individuals in such a society find themselves

performing functions not participated in by all the people around them, the vocabulary begins to reflect the differences in role. Medicine men, shamans, warriors, priests, and others develop special skills, and their language, usually still unwritten, may at this time begin to differ from that of fellow-tribesmen.

If, in addition to a diversity of roles, the members of the group find themselves on different caste or class levels, higher than some and lower than others, this too reflects itself in speech. The nobleman and his family may utilize methods of discourse different from those of serfs and peasants; certainly there is a great diversity between the language of property-owner and slave.

Class language was in use in human societies long before the lads of Cambridge and the busmen of London were talking to each other with the greatest of effort. Even hunting and gathering tribes in North America, living on what is now the Northwest coast of the United States, had a highly differentiated class language in a relatively small society.

Language that is dissimilar from one social or economic class to another begins to develop in two major directions: the noble and the vulgar. Because the latter is considered low-class and unacceptable, it becomes the repository for forbidden words, verbal taboos, foul language banished by the elite from the tongue of propriety.

Taboo has a powerful and magiclike quality over a community. If the name of an animal is banned from a language because the word resembles the name of a person who has died, no member of the community is permitted to violate the law. One may not speak the forbidden word; one may not even think it, just as mother, teacher, or religious counselor admonishes the child not to think dirty words.

In a highly stratified society, the taboos become a reflection of the manner in which the society is categorized; they are an instrument by which one may recognize class differences; and they are one of several means by which the class differences are reinforced.[25]

Stratification is not only the result of divergent educational achievement, but is itself the cause of different educational opportunities. Thus the speech of the lower and higher economic groups continues to diverge.

With little schooling given to workers, peasants and soldiers, not to mention serfs and slaves, a language develops among these people noticeably different in grammar, syntax, vocabulary, and pronunciation from that of the upper or ruling groups.

The cleavage widens. The mode of speech and of writing of the educated upper stratum finds its way into laws, books, university lectures, while workers on their jobs and in their homes, with little literacy and almost no contact with the upper group, develop a language of quite a different character.

Pronunciation differs widely under these circumstances, and words are used that are not acceptable to the official overseers of the purity of the tongue. The words may be merely quaint or outrageously dirty. Without the benefit of the printed word, they manage to display virility. They diffuse rapidly, have the toughness to survive, and become a universal part of the permanent yet tabooed language.[26]

FIVE

ROM ungrammatical constructions to forbidden words, a shadow language, an outlawed language, thrives. It takes on many shapes and forms, serves many purposes, and seems to be classifiable into six groups, more or less discrete, that overlap only slightly:

1. *Unaccepted, ungrammatical, uneducated speech:* These are the signs of the lower-income groups in a society in which the high-income groups establish an intellectual oligarchy.

36

Ain't it so? or *he don't know better* are examples of this un-grammatical speech. People who develop their speech habits without benefit of formal education often invent words and expressions for clarity and lucidity. For example, in a language that does not use *thee* and *thou*, some speakers achieve clarity by adding the phoneme *s* (or *se*) to *you*, resulting in *yous* or *youse*, while others add the suffix *-all* to denote plurality: *you* would refer to one individual, *you-all* to several.

Particularly in America, and probably throughout the Western world, the gap between the educational levels of diverse socioeconomic strata narrows under the impact of a society having the great force of social mobility. As this occurs, in a land where millions are hearing the same speech at cinemas, over the radio, and on television, the ungrammatical area of outlawed language diminishes in importance.

2. *Idiom in the making:* These are the words and phrases that are neither blasphemous nor dirty, but have slanglike inelegance. They are homey expressions that have not gained wide acceptance by that amorphous and unofficial "academy" that seeks to rule the American language. *Money* has long been known as *dough,* and more recently as *bread;* if it is given as a bribe, it is *hush money;* if it is extra or unexpected, then the *dough* or the *bread* turns into *gravy.*

This area of slang is rich in expressions and phrases of a longer nature. A man might *make a splash,* or *have an ace in the hole,* or *have something up his sleeve,* or if he has an enemy, he *might set out to fix his wagon.*

3. *Speech of an isolated group, or of a group seeking isolation:* These are the areas of language known as cant or

jargon. In the catalogue of the New York Public Library, one finds entries for the slang of aviation, boxing, butchers, and the groups and professions continue alphabetically right down to students, transport workers, and vagrants, not to overlook chimney sweeps. There is a slang for railway workers and for actors, a slang for petroleum workers and for lumbermen.

In one of the many dictionaries devoted to American slang,[27] there is a specialized language for actors, advertising men, airmen, American soldiers in France, announcers, and so it goes, again alphabetically, and if the gamut is not covered from A to Z, it is only because the author could not find any groups in the X, Y, and Z categories. There is a special section devoted to slang of the opera, another for the slang of hoboes, of liquor, of marriage, ending with wrestlers and writers, and carefully excluding or overlooking excretion and copulation.

In some instances, jargon of a special or socially isolated group may serve the purpose of protecting the speakers from being understood by others. More often, it imparts an in-group identification to the users, a sense of belonging.

A dictionary devoted entirely to the slang of criminals (an example of specialization within specialization) contains words and phrases for almost every act, object and character-istic that might be encountered during criminal activity, a courtroom scene, or prison life.[28] Thumbing through such a dictionary, one can easily imagine a group of people hold-ing a conversation, freely communicating among themselves, while others present are as unable to follow the discussion as they would be if a foreign tongue were being used.

4. *Slang of ethnic slur*: This is the pejorative that arises

from racial and ethnic differentiation and intergroup conflict. This category of words and phrases (for which Roback coined the word *ethnophaulism*[29]) thrives in the United States even more than elsewhere, particularly because of the urbanization of the American society and the coexistence of discrete cultural groups within one social community.

Ethnophaulisms are not unique to the melting-pot society of America. They are found in all lands where they are weapons against foreigners. However, in a folk society, such types of words (particularly ethnic pejoratives), are less likely to be required. Although such a society would often experience a clash of tribes (as in a war), the two or more peoples usually would not coexist over a period of time in very close proximity without becoming assimilated into each other (hence forming a new group) or without one becoming extinct in favor of the survival of the other. However, such long-range coexistence of discrete cultures, even in simple societies, was not unknown.

In the United States, where men and women of diverse faiths and numerous origins live together with more proximity than assimilation, the ethnic epithet has become a significant part of the linguistic development. The Catholic, Protestant, and Jew; the Negro and the white; the immigrant and the native-born; the family of Italian descent and the family of Russian descent: in a heterogeneous society these groups retain their individual identity.

Where an individual has minority-group status, he is frequently described in an uncomplimentary manner, by the use of emotionally-loaded words that the official society frowns upon. As one might expect, the minority retaliates with similarly resented epithets against the majority. The Negro uses terms like *cracker* and *snake* as emotion-loaded retaliatory terms against the white.

5. *Speech of blasphemy and its corruption into nonprofane slang*: These are words and phrases in which the commandment that the Lord's name (and other ecclesiastical words) shall not be invoked in vain is either violated or avoided. New and phonetically related words and phrases come into the language to circumvent the blasphemy. The profanity or the curse takes the form of *God, Christ, Jesus, goddammit,* and the now mild *hell,* or the use of these and similar words in such longer phrases as *for Christ's sake* or *to hell with it.*

A modification of this slang takes place when the words cannot be stopped, but can be deprived of their religious blasphemy by some slight changes in the phonemes. *God* becomes *gosh, damn* becomes *darn,* and their joined form *goddammit* becomes *goldarnit. Christ,* standing alone, is easily transformed into *Cripes,* with phonetic similarity more striking than the orthographic dissimilarity; and *Well, for Christ's sake* becomes *Well, for kiss my ass.*

An examination of this last phrase and the more common *for crying out loud* reveals that they start with exactly the same sound formations as *for Christ's sake,* but the person uttering them is halted in this process before the name of Christ has been completed, and the blasphemer is thus saved from sin.

One avoids saying *Oh hell* or *hot as hell* (not to mention *cold as hell*) by transforming the *hell* into *heck*. Even *gee whiz* probably originated as a corruption of *gee ziz* which differs phonetically only in the most minute manner from *Jesus*. And the innocent sounding *Oh my* is the sinful *Oh my God*, from which the last syllable has been expurgated. [30, 31]

6. *The language of sex and excretion and of the organs of the body associated with these processes:* These are words that have come to monopolize the area of forbidden sounds in English, and that, almost without exception, have attained figurative (that is, nonbiological) connotations in addition to the literal (that is, biological) ones.[32]

If the prohibited sounds of blasphemy dominate the field of curse words (even the phrase is avoided: it becomes *cuss words*), so do those of sexual and excretory processes that of *dirty words*. This latter is a heading that is no doubt emotionally loaded, carrying an implication (one might, in fact, call it an explication) either that the words have a sordid uncleanliness as word sounds by themselves, or that they represent phenomena (objects and processes) that are sordid and unclean.

Nevertheless, *dirty words* seems to be the most accurate heading under which one subsumes the forbidden sound formations pertaining to these biological processes and objects, and extending to cover their use in figurative slang. As a heading, *dirty words* points quite clearly to the morphemes under consideration and at the same time expresses modern cultural attitudes toward parts of the body and the functions they perform.

Except for *dirty words* or the synonymous *obscene words*

(the two mean approximately the same thing, and the former is more satisfactory because it is more forthright, less euphemistically evasive), there is no general descriptive phrase in English which describes the commonly used terms for excretion (*shit, piss, pea,* and phrases in which they are found); of sex (*fuck, screw,* and phrases in which these words occur); and of the organs of the body most directly concerned with these functions (*cock, prick, dick, balls, ass,* and several others, and the phrases employing these terms).

As a special area of English slang, these words are rich and colorful. Walt Whitman, the bearded sage who has been made into an American folk-hero, said, "Many of the slang words ought to be collected—the bad words as well as the good—many of the bad words are fine." [33]

Shocking and tabooed, these words are nevertheless employed with the greatest of frequency. If one focuses attention particularly on the nonbiological uses of these words and phrases, perhaps one can utilize this aspect of our language (and hence of our culture) to demonstrate how, as Sapir stated, language "powerfully conditions all our thinking about social problems and processes." [34]

2 *The Handwriting on the Wall*

SIX

ECAUSE certain words carry a deep social stigma, it does not follow that they should be ignored by the student of language," wrote Read.[1] Let us start, then, by analyzing the words that carry the stigma.

The processes, products, and organs of excretion and of sexuality have given rise to a language that can be described under several different headings:

1. *The official and accepted language:* These words are

usually little used outside of medical and juridical circles, although sophistication has brought some of them into more common usage than hitherto.[2]

Under this heading, one would place *copulation, cohabitation* (a euphemism in origin), *fornication* (with specialized meaning, in which it is reserved for the illicit), *ejaculation, erection, tumescence, detumescence, semen, penis, testicles, urethra, vagina, scrotum, urination, micturition, defecation,* and *feces,* among many others.

Some of these words are today generally understood by a wide public; perhaps this can be said of all of them with the exception of *micturition* and of *tumescence* and its antonym. But most of these words are little used in conversation. Because there are other forms of speech at hand, they somehow appear to be prudish, clumsy, or long, even when they are easy to say and rather short. They appear to be awkward for the free flow of easy speech, although it is certainly less awkward to speak of *defecation* than of *sitting on the potty.* With the exception, perhaps, of *penis,* these words have found their way only to the most limited extent into the everyday language of the people.

Thus, a mother can speak to her child about *his penis,* but would hardly teach him how and when *to defecate.* The latter, like most words in this category, is inadequate because it appears artificial and unappealing, and hence unlikely to be widely used in ordinary conversation. But it has an aura of artificiality not because of any inherent structure of the word, not because of length or meaning, but because it is given that connotation by those who use it and those who avoid it.

It would be difficult to have a prolonged discussion of sexuality, outside of medical and legal circles, in which the vocabulary centers around *copulation* and *cohabitation*.

2. *Longer but less technical words and phrases:* Entirely accepted, universally understood, these words are usually even clumsier than the more forthright medical terms. Perhaps the most common is *to have sexual intercourse,* sometimes shortened to the form *to have sex.* Correspondingly, for the excretory process, one speaks of *moving the bowels* or *having a bowel movement.*

It is difficult to imagine a man sitting with his ladylove and asking her: "Honey, will you have sexual intercourse with me now?" Nor would *copulate* or *fornicate* be more adequate, and he would be most unlikely to suggest to her: "Let's commit adultery, sweetie, what do you say?"

3. *Euphemisms and evasions*: These are words and phrases in which the direct mention of the process or object is avoided, and sometimes the very opposite is stated. The concept is implied, but the harshness is somewhat alleviated by the linguistic form. Euphemism seems to be an almost universal phenomenon. "In the popular speech of many nations," wrote Jespersen, "are found instances of a peculiar class of round-about expressions, in which the speaker avoids the regular word, but hints at it in a covert way by using some other word." [3]

This is a particularly large group of words and phrases, of which a few examples will suffice for the moment: *to go to bed with, to sleep with, to sleep around, to do it, to make love,* are some of the sexual terms. Likewise described euphemistically is excretion: *to do your duty, to make water, to make weewee,* or just plain *to make.*

The euphemisms abound for parts of the body (as *the organ* and *the privates*), and for the place where excretion takes place (*the toilet* becomes *the bathroom,* even in a public building where there is no bath, and where the one thing it is not is a bathroom).

4. *Dirty words:* These are the most common, the most harsh, the easiest to say and, until recently, the hardest to print.

The medical terms, the clumsy phrases, and the euphemisms are all inadequate for everyday speech. They cannot suffice for unstilted conversation among peoples, for a free communication of thought, or even for the inward thought process in which one verbalizes to oneself. Simple words are required, and if they were not available (as once they were not) they would have to be invented.

Usually monosyllables, sometimes of four or five or even six letters, they are referred to as *four-letter words,* a generic title which is itself significant because it is an evasive euphemism.[4]

Often originating in Latin and coming to English through the Romance tongues, these are referred to as Anglo-Saxonisms, again an evasion and an historical simplification, if not an inaccuracy.[5]

In some instances, these words are unquestionably the sole vocabulary that many people have at their command to describe the processes and objects. In every instance, from peon to President and from quean to queen, all those for whom the English language is a native tongue have these words at their command. They are necessary to the vocabulary of those whose total range of word power measures only a few hundred, and those for whom the number soars to tens of thousands.

Thus one does not require *copulate* in a vocabulary that contains *screw* and *fuck*; one does not have to speak of *the penis* and *the testicles* or learn about *the scrotum* when the vocabulary has *prick, cock,* and *dick* (synonymous to the point of being interchangeable), as well as *balls* and *nuts*.

In this vocabulary, one does not *ejaculate;* the verb is *to come* or *to shoot.* There is no gap in the vocabulary for the millions who never heard of *tumescence,* for they know the meaning of *hard-on* when they do not think in terms of *erection.* As for *detumescence,* there are some phrases in existence (as *go limp* or *go flat*), but little use is made of these mildly forbidden terms, perhaps because users of this language never find themselves in such a state or, if they did, they would certainly not wish to talk or think about it.

One does not have to say that he has *to defecate* or *to have a bowel movement;* it is so much easier (verbally, at least, although not in the world of material reality) *to take a shit,* or just *to shit,* while the noun (identical with the verb) is substituted for the more awkward *feces. Urination* is easy to avoid as a word, if not as a process; the commonly used term, verb or noun, process or object, is *piss.*

This language is clear, it is meaningful, it is accurately descriptive and satisfactorily easy to use. Given the attitudes in Western society toward the biological processes which it describes, it was inevitable that the outlawed language, the vulgar tongue, should have arisen. It came into being under the special conditions that were associated with the aura of privacy, guilt, and shame surrounding the processes and the products thereof.

However, what seems to have been investigated but little in the past is that these monosyllabic morphemes found their way into the language in contexts completely devoid of any sexual or excretory association. Almost without exception, they are commonly used in nonbiological connotations. Both as single words and in longer phrases, they are employed in a figurative manner, with emotional tones, feelings, and meanings that can shed considerable light on both language and culture.

SEVEN

INASMUCH as certain parts of the body are primarily used both for excretory and sexual purposes, there is a physiological association between the two processes. In that one discards from life and the other generates new life, there is a juxtaposition of the two on opposite ends of the life process. One is the beginning, the other is the end.

What does the language of excretion tell us about Western culture? There is no language of defecation that is not either clumsy or embarrassing, on the one hand, or proscribed and dirty on the other. Setting aside for the moment the discussion of the organs involved (which shall be studied separately at a later point) the key words in this language are *shit,* both as verb and noun, and *piss,* again used for both parts of speech.

Despite the attribution of all monosyllabic dirty words (particularly those that happen to contain exactly four letters) to the Anglo-Saxons, it would seem that there is some dispute on whether they deserve credit for either *piss* or *shit,* which have on various occasions been traced to Old English, modern Dutch, Old French, Latin, and other sources.[6]

The French commonly use such words as *pisser* and *pissoir,* and the French verb for *shit* is *chier* (the world-renowned noun, *merde,* seems to have had no influence on English linguistic evolution). The close association of *shit* and *chier* is heard when French and English are pronounced together, for both start with the same *sh* sound, represented by the same phonetic symbol.

Possibly *piss* has an onomatopoeic origin. It would seem that the sound suggests the process, although this is frequently difficult to determine without a cross-cultural linguistic study, for once one has a clear-cut association of the sound and process, one finds the process in the sound, whether or not it is actually there. "The origins of human speech," wrote a pioneer linguist, Paget, are so remote that "it would be unreasonable to expect to find, now, any traces of the original sounds." [7]

Pea or *pee* seems to be a shortening of *piss,* and has euphemistic overtones. There may be here an effort to avoid the full impact of a dirty word by only mentioning the naughty letter with which it begins. Berrey and Van den Bark, in their dictionary, cite the form *P*, as well as *pea* or *pee*, thus substantiating this suggestion of the origin.[8] Recently, the new Merriam Webster unabridged dictionary suggested that *pee* is the first letter of the more forbidden *piss*.[9] The form *peepee* is also a milder manner of saying *piss*, with repetition of the monosyllable giving a baby-talk tone to the word, and thus cushioning its impact as a vulgarism.

The use of an initial or a series of initials to avoid dirty words has become quite widespread, as we shall see later. It is a manner of suggesting an idea, without enunciating it, and even takes hold where the full word or phrase is not prohibited, but is too explicit.

Thus, the mother who exhorts her child *to have a bowel movement* ends by teaching him *to make B.M.*, and then refers to the feces itself as *B.M.*, although it is not a movement, but the product of the movement.

If the circle is completed and if it repeats the history of *piss* becoming *P* and then *pee*, we may end up with a slang word *beeyem*, somewhat euphemistically synonymous with *shit*, and its users might well be unaware of an origin or an association with two initials.

Although the words *shit* and *piss* are universally understood and instantly identified with the processes and products of excretion (defecation and micturition, respectively), they are both used, the former more than the latter, in a wide variety of nonbiological senses. "The verb dates from ca. 1300," writes Eric Partridge about *shit*, "the noun from ca.

1500, since when, indeed, it has been a term of contempt for a man." [10]

By itself, *shit!* is an expletive, not an imperative, and foreign-language equivalencies for *shit,* such as the French *merde,* seem likewise to have two usages, literal and figurative, or biological and nonbiological, with no ambiguity resulting therefrom.

Standing alone, or uttered in such an expression as *Oh, shit!* the word has no suggestion of command. There is no understood *you* in such a sentence. The maiden teacher in the fourth grade of elementary school, teaching her children to parse the sentence, even one as short as *Go!,* would not contend that *Shit!* is a verb preceded by an understood second person pronoun as subject.

Rather she would see *Shit!* like *Merde!* as a word of frustration, of disgust, of dismay or unhappiness. By itself, and in this form, its meaning is entirely free from biological connotations. This use of the word (in English and French) is repeated in many modern languages, where the closest equivalent of *shit* or *to shit* is used in a figurative sense as an expletive of disgust.

Used with extreme frequency is the phrase *tough shit,* which means that something is *just too damn bad,* a somewhat stronger method of saying *tough luck,* from which it may trace its descent. But whereas the latter would be used by an individual to describe his own unfortunate fate, the former is contemptuously thrown, in an atmosphere of defiance, at another person.

Thus, *tough shit* is an adaptation of *tough luck* in a

sentence in which the words *that's your* (preceding) or *for you* (following) are explicitly stated or implicitly understood, as the case may be. But one would never speak of oneself as running into *a bad streak of tough shit,* although a man might well bemoan his own *tough luck.*

One frequently encounters the initials *T.S.,* used as a foreshortened and more respectable form of *tough shit.* There is another important idiom, *tough sledding,* likewise represented by the same initials, and the two phrases have somewhat similar meanings. It is difficult to know which was the earlier phrase, but it was probably *tough sledding,* which changed to or was largely replaced by *tough shit* as part of the generally universal dissemination of tabooed language prior to and especially during the Second World War.

What is of interest here is that the abbreviations of forbidden words and phrases require for their own standing and respectability other and more acceptable antecedents. Whichever comes first, two phrases are needed for a single set of initials. This will be apparent when we consider *T. S.* in conjunction with *snafu, S.O.L., PO.'ed,* and others.[11]

There are many longer phrases in which the word *shit* is found. Consider, for example, *he is full of shit,* which simply means that *he is a liar,* that *he is telling an untruth. I will knock the shit out of you* means that *I will impose physical violence upon you. To make shit out of someone* means to *subject another to crushing humiliation.*

Thus far, all of the examples of nonbiological uses of the word express negative or undesirable qualities. To continue: *a person is up shit creek* (often used in the slight variation, *up shit's creek*) when *he is in an untenable position*, and when this position has worsened to the point where there is superlative (or exaggerated) emphasis on this untenability, then *he is up shit's creek without a paddle*.

In a very simple way, *shit* is made into an adjective by adding *ty: shitty*, which describes anything having undesirable qualities. One makes a *shitty* speech, or a lad might complain that *he took a shitty course in college*.

The word *shit* finds its way into numerous synonyms for reprobate: he is *a shit-ass, a shit-heel* or (according to Berrey and Van den Bark) *a shote* or *a shoat*.[12]

Contempt for the biological process is expressed in the phrase *holy shit,* an exclamation of surprise in which the aura of the sacred is imparted to the repulsive. Precisely because it is *shit,* it cannot be *holy*: the phrase thus brings together the most incongruent of phenomena.

The *shit-list* has several related meanings, all descriptive of equally undesirable characteristics. A person is *on your shit-list* if *you don't like him,* or if *you are holding something against him*. In this sense, it is a figurative, personal blacklist.

In a more literal sense, the *shit-list* is in fact synonymous with *blacklist*. In Naval slang, it is said to be the *delinquency list*. In union and other working group circles, it is the list of people about to be laid off the job.

To be *shit out of luck* is to be *unlucky,* in fact very unlucky, a commonly used phrase occasionally shortened to *S.O.L.,* which in turn requires a respectable antecedent, namely *short of luck* or *sure out of luck*.

Although little used in contemporary English, a word

cited by Mathews' *Dictionary of Americanisms*[13] is *shitepoke,* defined as *a term of opprobrium,* and the dictionary gives the derivation of the first syllable as coming from "the vulgar word for excrement." The word is also used in another negative sense, in the phrase: *as crazy as a shitepoke.*

In certain instances, the negative character of the phrase may not be quite as apparent. There is the frequently uttered: *I don't give a shit,* meaning *I don't care.* In fact, so little do I care that I do not even give up the most worthless of all objects.

An expression found in Capt. Grose's original work, one of the most important in the history of slang dictionaries, is *sh-t sack,* described as *a dastardly fellow,* or alternatively, as *a nonconformist.*[14] In a very modern slang dictionary, and probably the most complete, that of Wentworth and Flexner,[15] there are numerous phrases and idiomatic expressions containing *shit,* and negative characterization runs through all of them. In Farmer's classic work,[16] which goes back to the late Victorian era, *shit* was a word of "violent abuse," likewise "a dastardly fellow."

Somewhat on the affirmative side, it might appear, is the expression *to shit a smoke,* meaning *to take a smoke in the men's room.* Here, however, *shit* is being used in its literal and biological sense. The idiomatic slang is an accordion-like collapse of a larger sentence, with the understood words being shown parenthetically: *to* (take a) *shit* (and in this way sneak) *a smoke.*

In our search for expressions in which *shit* is used affirmatively in a figurative manner, we have come across some examples of Army slang. Roast beef hash, Berrey and Van den Bark state,[17] is referred to as *buzzard shit,* and when served on toast as *shit on shingles,* abbreviated to the ever-popular *S.O.S.* While eating cannot be considered a repulsive act, the soldiers who developed this terminology used it to express their contempt (real or pretended) for Army food. On examination, the expressions are hostile to the food and hence to the Army, and general antipathy toward the Army is expected to be expressed by all enlisted men, particularly in what Riesman terms an "other-directed" society in which people try to be what their peer group expects them to be.

In French, the word *chier* is likewise used in a nonbiological and figurative manner. One of the most insulting remarks that a person can make to another in French is: *tu m' fais chier,* and although literally it can be translated as *you make me shit,* the connotation is better expressed in English by *go fuck yourself.* Instead of calling on sex for the source of the insult, the French call on excretion. One of the older French-English dictionaries[18] translates *vous me faites chier* as *you bore me,* and *chier du poivre* as meaning *to abscond,* both being negative qualities.

Somewhat less prohibited, somewhat less unspeakable and unprintable in proper books and in polite society, yet far from being accepted into the language, is *crap,* probably the best-known synonym for *shit.* In its biological meaning, it is interchangeable with *shit,* particularly in the phrase *to take a crap,* although it is only rarely used as a verb, *to crap,* and not infrequently as a noun.

Like *shit,* the word *crap* has its nonbiological meanings in the shadow language, and these connotations for the two words are remarkably similar. This is particularly true where mendacity is involved. If someone makes a factual statement that challenges the credulity of the listener, the latter might simply remark, *Crap,* or *that's crap,* or very likely, *you're full of crap,* to denote that he regards the speaker as having made serious departures from objective truth.

In another sense, *crap* is almost anything dirty, disarranged, unpleasant. The executive who walks into his office and, in dismay, sees a desk cluttered with papers, may ask his secretary: *What's all this crap doing here?* If rephrased: *What's all this shit doing here?* the same connotation is communicated, but with a slightly harsher emotional tone.

The dual use of tabooed words in both their literal and figurative meanings has been a difficulty confronting the adult seeking to learn English for the first time, and often finding himself in puzzling, amusing, and embarrassing situations. Witness, for example, this report of a young Dutchman in England, the son of a famous Dutch historian, who was working hard at the task of acquainting himself with English customs and speech:

> I remember one occasion in particular. It is as painful to recall as it is difficult to relate without giving offence all over again. But even so I feel the dreadful story must be told so that it may serve as a cautionary tale for all those who are addicted to my particular form of snobbery. It happened at a time when I was feeling very pleased with the recent progress I had made in the conquest of the English gentleman's idiom and deter-

mined to show it off. In particular there was one expression whose mastery I was all the keener to demonstrate as it seemed to me so specially idiomatic. In fact, when I first heard the phrase it sounded so idiomatic to me that I could hardly believe my ears. "If any of you gentlemen would like to pump ship . . ." our host had said after we had finished the port. Only what I, mishearing the last letter, understood him to say was an infinitely more coarsely expressed offer of facilities for the performance of a closely related physiological function. It seemed unbelievably crude, especially coming from such a very distinguished old gentleman and after the very restrained conversation his age and rank had imposed on us young men during the stylish ritual of the slowly rotating decanter. But shocking as it might be, there was no doubt about it, I had heard what I had heard; the English gentleman's idiom was apparently an extraordinary mixture of Puritan reserve and Rabelaisian abandon.

And so I carefully committed the extraordinary phrase to memory, keen to make use of it at the first possible opportunity. It came only too soon, that same week, when I went to a dance given in a private house where the champagne flowed as freely as ever with the result that shortly after midnight I realised my chance had come. "Please, sir," I said to my host, who was something very high up in the Law and chatting with someone who looked like a bishop, "please, sir, could you tell me where I could pump . . .?" "I beg your pardon?" he said, while an expression of incredulous bewilderment mixed with extreme distaste clouded his handsome face, "what did you say?" I repeated the outrageous inquiry, articulating even more precisely and proudly than before. I need hardly relate what followed: two pairs of eyebrows arching till you could almost hear them bristle in the icy silence, two aquiline noses wrinkling with contempt, and then two erect backs turning upon me and striding away. It was all over in a matter of seconds. And so was my social career.[19]

EIGHT

IKE defecation, urination lends itself to a similar pattern of euphemisms and double-meaning dirty words. The mother who tells her little boy *to do his duty* when she is inducting him into our toilet-trained culture is the same woman who has the child stand up and *make weewee*.

It is amusing to conjecture on the origin of the word *weewee*, for it is a phrase that possibly may have come from the upper-class children whose French governesses were ex-

horting them to take an affirmative step in learning to urinate at the proper time and place. Unable or unwilling to
say *pisse, pisse, s'il te plaît,* they would avoid the word by saying (in French) *yes, yes,* which as every schoolboy knows, is
oui, oui. Did the latter then find its way into the English language as *weewee?* The question is posed, but not rhetorically,
for unfortunately there is no documentary evidence to sup-
port or repudiate this suggested etiology.

Inasmuch as defecation is above micturition on the hierarchy of socially unpleasant functions, it is natural that *shit*
should have been appropriated more than *piss* to express
concepts of unpleasantness in nonexcretory areas.

However, *piss* is by no means absent from this category. A
person says that *he is pissed off* to denote that *he is displeased*
or *unhappy* or *frustrated* about something. As *tough shit* is
expressed in the form of *T. S.,* so *pissed off* can be avoided by
saying *P.O. 'ed;* not as difficult in oral language as in written
form, these initials have become commonly used and almost
universally understood. Like the previous examples, *P.O. 'ed*
(pronounced *pee-ode,* or phonetically *pi `od*) requires a re-
spectable antecedent to which it may be attributed, and this
is *put out,* the analogue of *tough sledding.* Ironically, *put out*
itself has a special and none-too-respectable meaning in the
shadow language, where it is used to denote the act of a girl
who voluntarily copulates: *She puts out for everybody,* for
example.

Another use of the word *piss* is in the phrase *to piss away,*
which means *to fritter away, to lose something valuable by
wasteful and stupid action. He pissed away the fortune that*

he inherited from his father, one would say, and so well does this communicate how he behaved with the money left in his possession that it is unnecessary to seek more lucid phraseology to express the thought.

Or, one would say that a man came out of the Army at the age of twenty-four, refused to return to school, did not work, and just *pissed away the years until he was thirty-five.* Again, the meaning is unusually clear; one could not demand more of the function of words for the purpose of communication.

Perspiration, in a jocular slang, is sometimes referred to as *pisspiration*; to perspire becomes *to pisspire.* Thus one word expresses simultaneously a negative attitude toward two bodily functions.

In criminal slang, *the pisshouse* is *the police station,* negative in the context in which it is used. *Piss and punk* is given in a slang dictionary for *bread and water.* Here two negative words are combined in a single phrase. What little use is made of this expression, it indubitably refers to food given as punishment, or to grub used for lack of real and desirable food.

By itself, *piss* is inferior liquor, also known by the picturesque phrase of *panther piss,* the etymology of which has not come to the writer's attention.

Sometimes one encounters phrases in which the forbidden sounds have meanings that fall somewhat between their literal and figurative connotations. In such instances, the biological context is not completely lost, but the full phrase is idiomatic. For example, *he was frightened* becomes *he was shitting in his pants* or *he was shitting green.* In the first case, the act of defecation is involuntary when one is in a state of fright; however, it is not meant that this literally occurred. In the second case, the involuntary character of the act is expressed by the unreadiness of the feces, *green* being a synonym for unripe. In each instance, uncontrolled defecation is synonymous with fright.[20]

These expressions become particularly remarkable when contrasted with another synonymous phrase for expressing fright: *to be scared shitless.* The very opposite biological phenomenon takes place; the person is in such a state of fear that he is unable to defecate, voluntarily or otherwise.

The significance of these two examples might be found in this contrast. In order to express the quality of fright, the negative character of which is indisputable, one appropriates the word *shit* even in mutually exclusive and self-contradictory manner.

In still another example, one says of a person that *he is caught with his pants down.* By this is meant that *he is caught in the act,* but not necessarily the sexual or excretory act; rather in any act in which one does not wish to be apprehended (here equated with exposed). In a wider sense, *to be caught with one's pants down* might cover a situation in which one is simply unprepared for an event.

In all of these cases, the semi-literal, semi-figurative usage is negative. But combination of several of the forbidden words, in one short and pithy sentence, reaches the nadir of negativism when they can be interpreted simultaneously both in the literal and figurative sense, as in the illustration: *shit, piss, and corruption!* Here are summarized in three major words and a connective conjunction all the terms of filth and evil, of dismay and disarray, that one can find at a moment's command.

Let us look at the company in which *corruption* is here placed. The sentence has its total effect because it is stinking with redundancy. All three major words are meant to express a single thought; the total negative character is aggrandized by virtue of this repetition. It is as if the three substances are combined in a synergistically opprobrious system, rather than in an additive one.

NINE

HE MODIFICATION of sacrilegious blasphemy into mild and very polite slang has an analogue in terms derived from dirty words associated with the excretory process. We have already seen how *gosh* and *darn, cripes* and *for crying out loud,* found their way into the language. They remained slang, but gained in respectability, and so completely did they lose their association with profanity that they could even be uttered in classrooms and from pulpits.

In this system, the first phoneme is usually retained. It is just as one utters it, and is about to continue, that there is still time to save the day, twist the tongue, and finish the monosyllabic formation in an innocent manner.

Once the word *shit* had gained common usage as a non-biological expletive, to the point where it was the first sound formation to come to mind for almost any expression of dismay, there was a danger that it would be spoken in the wrong places, under the wrong circumstances, and in the wrong company.

There was a need, at this point, for another word, expressing the same thought and starting with the same phoneme. Two such words are commonly used, *shucks* and *sugar*.

Although both *shucks* and *sugar* have approximately similar standing from the viewpoint of propriety, the former is more acceptable because the populace is not as fully aware of its origin. It seems to have attained independent standing as an expletive of a mild character.

So respectable is *shucks,* in fact, that it can appear on the sports page of the *New York Times*, where there is no indication that its use in the context shown was most unlikely:

One of Gary Bell's pitches hovered a split second too long in Mickey Mantle's strike zone last night at the Stadium. Before the Cleveland right-hander had time to say, "Shucks, there goes No. 52," it was gone.[21]

Why is it that *sugar,* equally respectable if not more so, is much less acceptable than *shucks?* I would suggest that when one says *sugar,* the artificial evasion is apparent. The speaker

67

and listener want to avoid saying *shit,* but do not want to be aware of their deliberate effort at evasion. In this respect, *shucks* is successful, *sugar* is not. Hence, when the latter is spoken, there is a snicker, as if the naughty word had itself been said. There is a mild shock, but not the shock of hearing the obscenity; it is the reaction at the nonmasculine cowardice that refuses to utter it.

Sophisticated circles regard the idea of substitution for a dreadful word as being a sign of weakness and cowardice. It is "sterilized swearing," complains Robert Graves, "guaranteed nonalcoholic substitutes for the true wine." [22] The substitution is a symbol of the lack of masculinity. It is necessary because, under certain conditions, such as in the sports columns of the *New York Times,* the original expletive remains strictly forbidden. Therefore, the substitution is acceptable, provided one is unaware of it. *Shucks* is fine, but *sugar* is quite distasteful.

The hostile attitude toward the word *sugar* (and, as we shall see later, the sweetly-sickening *fudge*) is an index of the extent to which the tabooed language has been accepted by people who themselves are unaware of the implications involved in the development and usage of it.

As sophistication spreads and *shit* becomes almost pure English, one hears some very slight modifications in the pronunciation, that might be spelled out as *shoot, sheet,* and *shyte* (the latter to rhyme with *white*). These are found in circles that look with disdain upon *sugar,* but not in those that have accepted *shucks* into their everyday tongue. And why not *sugar? Great jumping beans, no!*

TEN

RAVELLERS in France and elsewhere on the European continent have seen the letters WC on narrow doors, and generally know that these initials stand for *Water Closet*. In order to denote that a room has been set aside for micturition and defecation, the French not only have recourse to foreign words, as unassimilated into their language as a phrase like *coup d'état* is into ours, but call into play a word that would never be used in an English-speaking country, and a letter and sound which are absent from common usage in their alphabet.

To express the fact that this is where one goes to defecate, the French put the letter *W* on the door, a letter that exists in their alphabet only as something belonging to the Germans or the English. This letter would not be found in a French dictionary if it were not needed for such words as *Washington*, *Waterloo*, and *water closet*.

In America, the embarrassment in the search for words that describe the place where one takes care of the excretory functions has produced some equally ludicrous situations. Mencken points out that it was the passage of the Comstock Postal Act, in 1873, that

> greatly stimulated the search for euphemisms. Once that amazing law was upon the statute-book and Comstock himself was given the inquisitorial powers of a post-office inspector, it became positively dangerous to print certain ancient and essentially decent English words. To this day the effects of that old reign of terror are still visible. We yet use *toilet, retiring-room, washroom,* and *public comfort station* in place of franker terms.[23]

Thus, according to Mencken, *toilet* came into the English language as a euphemism, simply because franker terms were frowned upon. But *toilet* itself has now completed a cycle. Children snicker as they put an I in the space between the two words on a sign that announces that a house or an apartment is TO LET. As it was used with greater frequency, *toilet* lost its euphemistic aura, acquired an air of vulgarity, and became a word not nice to say in proper company. Makers of perfumes have tended more and more to call their products colognes, rather than toilet waters, thus glossing over a real albeit slight technical difference between the two terms.

With *toilet* not quite proper, one hears a person saying that he has *to go to the bathroom,* although he knows that he is going to a room in which he will not bathe, and when in a public place, a room in which there is no bath.

The search for euphemy by modern man is evidently not satisfied by speaking of the bathroom when one means the toilet. Otherwise civilized men and women, almost as if they are mocking themselves (as indeed they may be doing), are now heard to say that they are going to *the little boy's room* or *the little girl's room.* Still others say: *I have to see a man about a dog.* To save us from this fate, there are *men's rooms, ladies' rooms, washrooms, rest rooms,* and *powder rooms,* and in England there are *cloak rooms,* all available for those who find *the toilet* too horrible to mention and who would rather die of constipation than go to *the shithouse.*

Today, people in nice company just cannot *go to the toilet,* any more than they can *go to the outhouse* or *shithouse.* Any word that directly points to the function for which the room is put aside is going to suggest more than that function; it will bring forth an image of all that is dirty, filthy, abhorrent, repellent, disordered, even in an upper-class home where the room shines with aseptic cleanliness.

This is precisely because words like *shit* and *shithouse* have been appropriated for figurative phrases in which the connotation of filth and disarray is used, and this connotation is reinforced in the mind of everyone speaking the language.

Not only is this true of the process that takes place in the toilet, but it is true of at least one synonym for the room itself. This is *can,* found in such expressions as *can it,* meaning *shut up, you're annoying me,* or *he got canned,* meaning that *he was discharged from a job.* The negative character of the non-biological term is apparent, but it is of unique interest in this instance, because *the can* is also physiological, it being synonymous with *the buttocks.*

An interesting use of slang to express the proper place for these biological processes is found in the word *head,* widely employed and having quasi-official standing in the language of the American Navy. The origin of the word seems to be traced to the place on the ship where the toilet is situated; namely, at *the head of the ship* (*the fore* or *prow* having long been called *the head*). It is possible that the word *head* was appropriated for this purpose by officers in order to have sailors avoid the use of a more unmentionable term.

In the context, *head* has a certain amount of respectability, and a person can say that *he is going to the head* (of the ship), hinting strongly at the reason for embarking on such a journey without actually verbalizing the forbidden intention, much as the child in school asks the teacher, *May I leave the room?*

Starting in this manner, the word *head,* in the Naval slang, soon loses all other meaning, and becomes a respectable method of saying that which one really should not say.

But for the population at large, this use of *head* is hardly well-enough known to solve the problem of the embarrassing gap in the language. *Toilet* is just not nice any more, and *bathroom* absurdly fails to state that which one wishes to communicate.

The language of slang therefore requires another short, simple term, preferably monosyllabic, not having unpleasant connotations, free from ambiguity, and having all the qualifications that make for quick and easy acceptance into the native tongue.

From time to time, over a period of centuries, the word *john,* or quite frequently *John* (perhaps in deference to the apostle) has been used as a polite synonym for the somewhat tabooed *toilet.* According to Mencken, it.was in the American women's colleges that *John* (or *Johnnie*) became the fashionable word, during the 1930's. In the preceding decade, at Vassar, the term was *Fred.*[24]

During recent years, it would seem that *john* has increased its popularity, and perhaps lost its preeminence as a capitalized (and hence proper) noun. Except for some young people who constantly announce that they are *going to the can,* most Americans in mixed company ask *where the john is* or say that that is where they are going.

If this widespread increase in usage continues, then one can predict that *john* will either become a dirty word, and may have to be replaced by *jay,* while male babies are no longer given a synonym for toilet as their Christian name; or it will make its way into full respectability, there will be a reaction against its use, and slang will again cry out for new words to fill the cyclically-recurring lacuna.

A prediction of this type is not difficult to make, when one studies the repetitive characteristics of certain linguistic phenomena. Consider what has happened to *toilet* in the light of this passage from the well-known work of Mario Pei, *The Story of Language*:

> The essential characteristic of euphemisms, whether arising from superstition or from other social reasons, is that in due course of time they lose their euphemistic character, assume the full, stark significance and connotation of the original word they have displaced, become taboo, and ultimately have to be replaced by new euphemisms.[25]

And for those who cannot imagine that people might stop naming their children *John* because of the embarrassment in the confusion with toilet, this passage from Randolph and Wilson is worth considering:

> Very strait-laced old-timers seldom name a boy Peter. I recall an evangelist from the North who shouted something about the church being founded upon Peter, and he was puzzled by the flushed cheeks of the young women and the ill-suppressed amusement of the ungodly. Another preacher, a real Ozark circuit rider, after talking about Peter's denial of Christ, suddenly shouted, "How many Peters air they here?" There was no laughter or snickering; the congregation was simply flabbergasted, and the poor preacher almost collapsed when he realized what he had said.[26]

ELEVEN

HUS, in two manners, our culture demonstrates its hostile attitude toward excretion. It uses euphemisms to avoid mention of forbidden words, utilizes initials, searches for foreignisms, and finds clumsy technical terms. And, second, it adopts (and adapts) the dirty words in the common language of excretion for nonexcretory purposes. and in so doing utilizes these words only to connote things of an undesirable character.

Whether we say *Shit!* as an expletive of disgust, or refer to *a liar* as being *a man who is full of shit;* whether we speak of disarray around a house as being *crap,* or a person who is dismayed as being *pissed off,* the pattern is the same. The forbidden biological words are used in nonbiological connotations almost invariably as the expression of qualities which are negative.

Excretion and the products thereof and the places in which it takes place are in this manner being described as filthy, disgusting, dirty, repulsive, and abhorrent. The hostile attitude of society first creates the forbidden language of dirty words and then the forbidden language re-creates and fortifies the hostile attitude.

The language is stating that the acts are improper, although unfortunately necessary, and the language properly reflects this impropriety. The culture looks upon the acts as dirty and the products of these acts even more so; and as part of this hostility it adopts the belief that this attitude is not imposed by society but exists as such in the nature of things. It is this situation which the language mirrors and at the same time perpetuates.

It is extremely rare to find the excretory terms adopted for figurative use to express qualities which are good, healthy, normal, pleasant, enjoyable, acceptable, or socially desirable.

The strong feeling of relief from tension that comes from the completion of a satisfactory defecation might, in a society that looked for the positive aspects of the excretory process, have been translated into the slang with the expression: *He is in the shithouse,* denoting that *he is out having a good time.*

Occasionally, however, one finds a suggestion of this in contemporary culture. The negative character of the figurative uses of the forbidden words is not without its exceptions. Deviant cases, though rare, do exist, although no such instance involving the word *shit* has come to this writer's attention.

A dictionary[27] cites the words *piss-cutter* and *piss-whiz* to describe a capable person; one who is no slouch. A small study made by this writer failed to uncover a single person who recognized the latter word or who recalled having heard it, and only a few who knew the former. To the extent that they are used at all, they are confined to a region or to an occupational or subcultural group, and the failure to diffuse throughout the English language might indicate that there is resistance in appropriating an excretory term for use in a complimentary fashion.

The word *piss-cutter* is recalled by some who served in the U.S. Marines during World War II. A Marine hat with an extraordinarily sharp edge—an edge so sharp that it could cut through a watery fluid like piss—was given this name. In its sharpness, this hat was exact, proper, *comme il faut,* and from this the generally affirmative usage may have been derived.[28]

A greater exception seems to be the word *pisser,* to denote a man or object of exceptional qualities. These unusual qualities may be negative or affirmative; to speak of something (or someone) as being *a pisser* only emphasizes the quantity of the quality, and does not necessarily impose a favorable value judgment on it. In this sense, the word may be said to be neutral.

There is another positive connotation in the expression *full of piss and vinegar,* in which the word represents strength, while *to piss through the same quill* is an old proverbial expression, used (according to the Oxford English Dictionary)[29] as far back as the eighteenth century; it refers to a state in which two persons are so intimate that they have no secrets from each other.

There is one extremely positive connotation in which defecation is sometimes found. It is in the form of an excerpt, taken out of context, from a well-known commercial slogan. Scrawled on the doors of toilets, one sees: *This is the pause that refreshes.* It is the youth and the little man expressing their defiance of big business in America—but is it also a portent of a new attitude making headway in our culture?

Is this the handwriting on the wall?

3

The Policy of the Big Stick

ROM excretion to the organs of the body concerned with this function is a step in the direction of greater taboo, because the external body organs that the layman identifies with the expulsion of waste matter are the same that he considers the most sexual, the most erotic.

In the development of cultural attitudes toward excretion, it is likely that this duality of functions served to assist those evolutionary trends tending to regard all excretory functions as being inherently evil just as they are unfortunately necessary.

If it were not for the fact that the penis and vagina are used, rather than the throat and mouth, urination might be considered no more of a private and unspeakable process than expectoration; in fact maybe less so, for the latter is certainly not as much a sign of a healthy individual as is the former.

But the erogenous zones are those also of greatest interest to urinary and defecatory processes, with the exception of the breasts, which are highly erogenous and whose excretory function is of a minor character except during the period following birth.

It would be expected that the organs serving for these two processes would likewise be unmentionable, and would, in a society that frowns upon both highly tabooed activities, give rise to the same types of language that we have been discussing. This is, indeed, the case.

So unmentionable, in fact, are the organs that they are called *privates*, and no word could more clearly express the great weight of taboo against talking about such things. Nevertheless, talked about they are and must be, and hence, once again, there are the clumsy and technical and scientific terms, the circumlocutions and euphemisms and nice words that say something while really avoiding it, and the language that is as universally used as it is self-righteously denied entrance into our official tongue.

The chief organs involved are the penis and vagina, serving in the dual-function capacity; the rectum and anus, primarily excretory; and scrotum and testicles, primarily sexual; and finally the breasts, the nature of one's interest differing with age and other factors.

The word *penis* is of particular interest in a linguistic study. Until recent years, it was as little used as many another word in a somewhat technical lexicon, such as *copulation* and *cohabitation,* but not because it was long or clumsy. It was just not right to talk about such things, and if one violated the normative order, there was no reason to choose a disyllabic word when a very expressive monosyllabic one was at hand.

One just did not speak about the *penis.* Mothers turned their faces the other way and avoided mentioning such things when talking to their little boys. But sophistication seems to have made some headway, and parents consider an index of their own liberation the frequency with which the word finds its way into the vocabulary of their offspring.

Nevertheless, among a large part of the population, *penis* is just not said, and *testicles* and *scrotum* still hardly known, so again there is recourse to evasive euphemisms and tabooed language.

Of all the euphemisms used by the adult population, other than the aforementioned *privates,* one is particularly peculiar: the word *organ.* A man who *plays with his organ* in public is not likely, when this is reported to others, to be misunderstood. No one will imagine that the man has displayed unusual musical proclivities on a streetcorner. Furthermore, there will be no ambiguity with regard to the part of his body that he was touching; no one will believe that he had been playing with his ear, which is certainly a very prominent organ.

The use of the word *organ* to express not any organ but one particular organ is clearly the result of an unwillingness to mention the unmentionable. It is hinted at subtly, in a whisper, but the very unmentionability, in which the generic term for an entire class is used for one member of the class, shows the importance of the penis in a language formed by people frantically seeking to avoid its recognition.

The children who are brought up and trained *to make,* instead of *to urinate* or *to piss,* will insist on knowing what they call this very interesting part of the male body. For a brief time, girls are told nothing, and boys must be satisfied to learn that it is *your little thing, your thing, your weewee,* and so on.

All of these terms being awkward, the mother who has neither mastered *the penis* nor mustered the courage to acknowledge it, just avoids giving it a name. And when it comes to *the testicles* and *scrotum,* what can she say, for usually she is ignorant of the technical terms, while the word she is most familiar with is, for her, vulgar and dirty.

Having been kept in deliberate ignorance, and having been subjected to lies and evasions, the child learns at an early age that the organs in question have names that are easy to say, well understood, and highly forbidden.

The new words form what is called *the vocabulary of the street, the language of the gutter.* The child learns that in each phrase or word there is an emotionally-loaded characterization. The thing for which there is a special name is filthy, because the word itself is filthy. It is easily seen that the words cannot possibly have any dirtiness inherent in them; they obtain this characteristic by virtue of their being tabooed.

The child, however, is told: *Don't use these words because they are dirty.* The effort exerted at a later date by parents and society to explain that the objects for which these words stand are clean, but only the words themselves are dirty, can have little impact upon the inculcated child.

For *the penis,* the child early learns that there are many substitutes, of which *prick* is the most common, with synonyms including *cock* and *dick.* MacDougald [1] has called attention to the plethora of forbidden words in which the monosyllable ends with the phoneme *k,* and has suggested the possibility of a physiological association. The question of whether a sound formation, caused by a physiological movement of mouth, throat, jaw, teeth, tongue, and other parts of the anatomy, can be correlated with concept or meaning, was investigated at some length by Paget,[2] and before him was suggested by the illustrious co-founder of the theory of evolution, Alfred Russel Wallace.[3] No definitive evidence has been gathered, but further study should be made of the place of the *k* sound in the sexual slang of English and other languages.

To return to the body, for the testicles and scrotum (either or both, for the differentiation is not made by users of this slang) there is one universal substitute: *balls.* For the female organs, the most common words are *cunt* and *pussy,* and turning over the body (of male or female) there are, in order of diminishing unmentionability, *ass, can, behind, backside,* and even *derrière,* which Bonwit Teller found respectable enough for an advertisement, the *New York Times* found fit to print,[4] and H. L. Mencken found worthy of being immortalized as a footnote.[5] And indeed immortal it should be made, for it is seldom that one finds an American department store appealing for the patronage of women with *fat asses,* even if they are referred to as *large derrières.*

Derrière might have been very convenient in the vocabulary of the soldier whose story is narrated by Robert Graves. Shot in the buttocks, he was asked by a visitor where he had been wounded, and could only reply, "I'm so sorry, Ma'am, I don't know: I never learned Latin." [6]

THIRTEEN

ET US dispose first of the scrotum-testicles amalgam. The word is *balls,* commonly used almost without embarrassment in a context having to do with round spherical objects, particularly when they appear as paraphernalia in a sporting event.

When employed in the singular, *ball* loses all of its significance or emotional tone as a dirty word, and fails entirely to communicate any thought related to the unmentionable parts of the human male body. Although *testicles* has a singular form, this is not true of *balls*.

Thus, one can speak of a person as standing *on the ball of his right foot*, but try to keep a straight face when someone says he is standing *on the balls of his feet*. Many people find it easy to go through life with *Ball* as the surname, but examination of telephone directories failed to uncover the name *Balls*.

People can refer to the Smith family as *the Smiths*, but Mr. and Mrs. Jonathan Percy Ball and sons are not known as *the Balls*. In fact, the writer heard of one gentleman whose name consisted of the letters Balze, which he carefully printed on his card as Balzé, and just as carefully enunciated in such a manner as would avoid any ambiguity. There are many names suggestive of obscenities and unmentionables, and sooner or later the offspring succumb to social pressure and effectuate a change. Once, it is said, there were many *Outhouses* in the U.S.A.; if any such families are to be found, they have not appeared in several major telephone directories that I have examined. And so it is with *Balls*. The suggested obscenity is all too apparent, despite the very proper connotation of the word, particularly in the singular.

The significant differentiation between *ball* and *balls,* it might be expected, would be reflected in the slang. This is true, with *ball* being used in affirmative qualitative descriptions, and *balls* (with one exception) in negative ones.

To indicate that a person assumes responsibility on a particular issue, it is said that *he carries the ball*. In a similar manner, *he is on the ball* if he is exceptionally alert; if the alertness is combined with a great deal of energy, the person is *a ball of fire.*

Because of the strong sanction against the use of dirty words in figurative but favorable connotations, it has become almost impossible to make a plural form for these expressions. One might say that a man takes on many responsibilities, yet it would be ludicrous to say that *he is on the balls* or *is carrying the balls.* In a very specific connotation, particularly where the literal meaning is used and the reference is to a sporting event, *balls* changes its character and loses its suggestion of taboo. For instance, a man can be juggling the balls. But in idiomatic, figurative speech, the plural refers to a part of the male anatomy.

The most common of all synonyms for *balls* in the vernacular is *nuts.* Like the former, it is employed to denote testicles only in the plural.

In the figurative sense, both of these words have similar meanings. As an expletive, *Balls!* or *Nuts!,* sometimes preceded by *Oh,* is a rather weak expression of dismay.

In another contextual framework, *nuts* is synonymous with a mental state that ranges anywhere from foolishness to lunacy. *You're nuts* means that *you are out of your mind,* not in the sense of being insane, but having come to a wrong conclusion or having made an improper decision.

Insanity, as a state, is expressed in the slang in many other ways, although the generally enlightened attitude toward mental health is causing a decline in the respectability of any slang word to describe such a condition.

When *nuts* or *nutty* is employed as somewhat synonymous with lunacy, it would seem to find its closest approxima-
tions in such other proscribed words as *bats, batty,* or the
unacceptable diminutive of lunatic, *loony.* But to speak of a
man as *being a nut,* or as having *gone nuts* or of *being nutty,*
while it may in a given context carry the implication of a state
of insanity, usually would not be so interpreted. However,
to call a given place *a nut house* would leave little room for
ambiguity.

The use of the word *nuts* to denote foolishness or stupidity is indeed commonplace and may increase in years to come,
but the use to denote insanity will continue to diminish. In
this instance, the changing character of the implication probably does not have its genesis in any watered-down meanings
that might result from the high degree of frequency of these
terms in an unrestrained and unconfined vernacular, but
rather to the growing sympathy of the public toward those
suffering from mental ailment.

As a synonym for insanity, *nuts* has thus fallen into a
new form of disrepute, the result of the intellectual disrespectability of antagonism toward mental derangement. This is
an attitude that rapidly causes linguistic change. It seeps
quickly down to large areas of the general population, after
only a brief cultural lag that in our era is frequently cur-
tailed by television, newspapers, and other media of mass
communication in a highly-urbanized propaganda-conscious
social milieu.

The hostile attitude of the social order toward sex is so

strong that a new form of taboo or restriction arises; namely, that one may not cast reflection on the mentally ill by describing their condition in terms derived from human anatomy.

One of the more interesting things that happened to the expletive *Nuts!* is its change to *Nerts!* This, of course, is in keeping with *God* becoming *gosh* and *shit* becoming *sugar.* The transformation of *nuts* to *nerts,* Mencken states,[7] originated in Hollywood, at a time when forbidden words were gaining in frequency of use in the movie colony. A movement was initiated to change the vowels of the words to *e,* followed by an inserted consonant *r.* If there were other examples, as *shert* or *ferk,* they have not survived, and no verbalized evidence that they ever existed has come to this writer's attention.

Today, however, *nerts* is frowned upon by a society that can accept *shucks* but not *sugar,* a society that is unwilling to face the reality of its own euphemistic escapisms, and wants them hidden a little more cleverly from itself.

But whatever happens to the word *nuts,* whether it remains *nuts* or becomes *nerts,* whether it is used colloquially with regard to the mentally ill or this meaning is entirely lost to our evolving tongue, the word itself, in its nonbiological meaning is, like *balls,* invariably negative. Be it simple dismay or utter lunacy, *nuts* is not a complimentary term.

An illustration of the double meaning of the word *balls* is found in a little story, oft-retold, of the queen who was lamenting her fate as second in command. "Balls!" said the queen, "if I had them I'd be king," and the king laughed, *not because he wanted to but because he had two.*

The humor in this anecdote is better preserved in oral narration, or might be expressed in phonetic symbols without losing any of its flavor.

Neverthless, one cannot depart from this area of the anatomy without stumbling across another deviant case, at least as significant as the aforementioned *pisser*: namely, *he's got balls,* a complimentary term that is approximately the equivalent of *he's got guts.* Unlike the negative slang, *he's got balls* is almost unknown to middle- and upper-strata economic groups, and its use is largely confined to adolescents, students, and personnel of the armed forces.

The phrase may be derived from the Spanish, where an expression of which this is a literal translation: *¡Que cojonudo es!* is heard with great frequency, particularly when the courage of a bullfighter is being emphasized. A somewhat similar expression: *¡Que huevudo es!* would be the equivalent literally to *you have nuts,* which does not have a figurative meaning. The *huevudo* in this phrase comes from *huevos,* a mild word for testicles, which in the nonbiological context means *eggs.*[8]

Spanish provides one example of the simultaneous use of tabooed language for anatomical description and figurative expression that has no equivalency in English. This is the word *pendejo,* which literally refers to the pubic hair, but more accurately might be translated more or less as *nincompoop,* the negative character of which is apparent.

Nevertheless, how can one explain the few exceptions, in English, Spanish or other tongues, as in the expression: *you have balls.* Perhaps, in this instance, there is attributed to the individual an anatomical organ of masculinity to symbolize a qualitative characteristic, courage—a trait that modern society (largely male-dominated) equates with masculinity.

FOURTEEN

N THE nonanatomical uses of the tabooed vocabulary, the penis and the rectum play a similar function, with the former stronger in tone than the latter. In each instance, the dirty word, instead of being used to describe a part of a person, is used to personify the individual and his entire being.

One says, for example, that *he is an ass,* meaning that *he is a fool, a damn fool at that.* But when we say that *he is a prick* (or, sweet irony, that *she is a prick!*), we express more than contempt for a person's judgment. We characterize that individual as being loathsome, abhorrent, and having repulsive qualities.

The individual who is *a prick* may also be *a fool,* in which case he would be *an ass,* but the state of *prickicity* (or *prickiness*) may have come about through cunning, craftiness, slyness, or cupidity, rather than through stupidity, in which case such *a prick* could never be *an ass.*

In England, where the slang is not exactly synonymous with that of the American language, the word *bum* is used as a proscribed synonym for *ass,* and the same word describes an undesirable person, who may be lazy, dirty, or generally good for-nothing.

Under certain circumstances, the word *ass* is synonymous with *luck,* with *good fortune.* This usage seems to be confined to the game of pool and billiards and to other activities around the areas where these games are played. Although no instance of similar usage in other sports has come to the writer's attention, such linguistic diffusion would not be unexpected.

In the poolroom, one says of a player who is lucky that *he's got ass,* or *he's got plenty of ass.* At first glance, this might be an example of a desirable quality, of the use of the word affirmatively, similar to the previously cited *he's got balls.* Further investigation reveals, however, that it is employed to state that the player has achieved his excellent results through chance or luck, not through talent or skill. If *a man has ass* in this sense, *he is lucky,* specifically meaning that *he is not talented.* It is actually a disparaging remark.

A similar connotation is implied in the adjective *assy*, to describe either an individual or his accomplishments. Although the word is not confined to athletic events, an illustration recently heard on the baseball field serves as an excellent paradigm, because the word was used to describe both the person and his achievement as a result of a single event. A batter connected with what looked like a home run, and the outfielder ran back and made an astonishing over-the-head catch while still running out at full speed. The batter, robbed of his hit, walked over to the sidelines and grumbled, *Boy, is he assy,* while at the same time a teammate of the batter remarked, *What an assy catch!*

In this example, *assy* has two possible meanings which are not clearly differentiated. The fielder can be said to have been *lucky* or *ostentatious,* or both. He might have been lacking in talent: hence he had good luck; or he might have made a grandstand play: hence he was a showoff. In either instance, the word is disparaging, and if the two possible meanings have a tendency to be mutually exclusive, this would not trouble the user.

Likewise in a disparaging manner, a girl is referred to as *ass* or as *a piece of ass,* to express that she is erotically desirable but romantically undesirable. She is a woman of acceptable body and unacceptable morals.

In still another connotation, *ass* means nerve: *it took a lot of ass to do that.* However, the implication is *lack of judgment.*

Summarizing, one finds that, in addition to the obviously negative meaning when one is called *an ass,* the word is used to express *luck, women,* and *nerve,* but—in the mind of the speaker—it is *luck without talent, women without morals,* and *nerve without courage.*

A common expression of mild contempt is *horse's ass,* which that inimitable collector of American folklore, Vance Randolph, found in this Ozarkian ditty:

Here's to the lass, and here's to the glass,
And both are fair to see;
But a lass's ass and a whiskey glass
Made a horse's ass of me.[9]

Like most of the previous words that have been discussed, *ass* is a legitimate and respectable word, it being synonymous with donkey, and many of the insulting and negative usages to which the word is put are derived from the animal, rather than from the part of the anatomy.

However, the etymology in no way modifies the current impact of the usage. Even if the language were originally a reflection of man's contempt for the donkey (and for other forms of animal life, as so much of our language so clearly shows), the impact of the idiomatic expressions, as used today, shows that the words are linked to human anatomy in the literal meaning, and to general repulsive qualities in the figurative.

It is in this light that one can understand two of the most common adjectives that are used to modify the nouns; namely, *big* and *perfect.* One speaks of *a big ass* or *a silly ass,* and the expressions may be akin to *a stubborn ass,* in which instance the donkey, and not the human buttocks, is the source for the phrase.

Whatever its origin, the expression today represents man's contempt for his own body, and not for an animal which is hardly known to millions of city dwellers. And when the same adjectives are used to modify *prick,* the meaning is clear. There is only slight difference between calling a person *a silly prick* and *a silly ass.*

Words lose their original meaning in the idiomatic phraseology of slang more quickly than in the accepted language of lexicography. Hence, it is not too surprising that *perfect* is employed to denote anything but perfection. One would hardly speak of a fool as having perfection; *the perfect ass* is the quintessence of a fool, he is more fool than just an ordinary fool. If one were to create a word in the manner that linguists call creolization, one might speak of him as being *assissimo.*

At one time, according to an author using the pseudonym of Justinian,[10] *prick* was encountered frequently with "opprobrious suffixes," such as *prick-face* or *prick-ears.* The latter may be ambiguous; at least one dictionary says that it refers only to the fact that the ears are longer than the hair.[11] These expressions do not seem to have survived.

As a modifier, *big* is somewhat more explicable than *perfect,* for it denotes dimensional qualities, in this instance in a figurative sense. *A big prick* is simply one with a great deal of *prickicity* about him; again, he is *much more prick* than *an ordinary prick,* although he may be very ordinary in many other ways.

97

It is a matter of more than passing interest that all these words are used only in a derogatory sense, whether as individual morphemes or as parts of phrases. Just as *shit* and *piss*, when unrelated to the excretory functions, express negative and hostile attitudes, so do *balls, ass,* and *prick*. The negative attitude may be one of frustration, disgust, or repulsion, but it is always an unhappy connotation. It is almost impossible, in fact, to imagine that such words might be used in a complimentary manner.

So ingrained is the method of imputing repulsive characteristics to the language of the genitalia that one finds it being done by Americans who speak foreign dialects and tongues. In Yiddish, for example, the word for *prick* is *shmuck,* and the latter is today almost universally understood by English-speaking peoples as synonymous with *fool*. That it can be enunciated in slightly more proper society is again a characteristic that it acquires from being a foreignism; in this instance, the foreign origin gives it a euphemistic quality, on the one hand, and suggests, on the other, that a speaker should go elsewhere (abroad or to other peoples) to find the dirty words.

FIFTEEN

HEN they have perfectly legitimate meanings, the naughty words prove very embarrassing to the language. Thus, many people avoid using the word *prick* in its acceptable and literal meaning; that is, the sensation of a pointed or thornlike object coming in contact with the skin. This may not in all instances be derived from prudery, for people who would avoid the accepted use of *prick* might use it frequently in prohibited anatomical and nonbiological slang.

The semantic factor is apparent, writes the linguist, Leonard Bloomfield,

> in the disfavoring of speech-forms that are homonymous with tabu-forms. . . . In America, *knocked up* is a tabu-form for "rendered pregnant"; for this reason, the phrase is not used in the British sense "tired, exhausted." In older French and English there was a word, French *con-nil, connin,* English *coney,* for "rabbit"; in both languages this word died out because it resembled a word that was under a tabu of indecency. For the same reason, *rooster* and *donkey* are replacing *cock* and *ass* in American English. In such cases there is little real ambiguity, but some hearers react nevertheless to the powerful stimulus of the tabu-word; having called forth ridicule or embarrassment, the speaker avoids the innocent homonym. It is a remarkable fact that the tabu-word itself has a much tougher life than the harmless homonym.[12]

Yes, good words fall into disrepute, while the tabooed words are tough and resistant. No matter how proper the original usage, once they are appropriated for illicit or unmentionable purposes, they are legislated by the hidden defenders of public morality out of the language of propriety.

"Even *bed* is not a term to be used by 'nice' girls before male strangers," write Randolph and Wilson about Ozark women. "Refined backwoods girls never 'go to bed'; they think it is more delicate to retire or even to lay down!" [13]

In a similar manner, an effort has been made to legislate the word *cock* right out of the English language, because of its being a synonym for *prick*. Once the farmers had hay-

cocks, where today they have *haystacks,* and the former term has all but disappeared. The *weathercock* became the *weathervane,* and the diminutive *roach* was used to replace the *cockroach.* Randolph says that in the Ozarks, people do not *cock a gun;* they *pull back both roosters!* They prefer to tell *rooster and ox stories* rather than *cock and bull tales.*[14]

Mencken cites an instance from a nineteenth century American novel, in which a young lad, delicately discussing some matters concerning the Navy with a young lady, referred to her brother as *roosterswain.* Let all those who utter *shucks* and *sugar* not laugh too loud at themselves upon reading this.[15]

It was the American campaign against the word *cock,* in fact, that caused Amos Bronson Alcox to change his name, and one might conjecture whether spinster schoolteachers and prudish librarians would have permitted *Little Women* and *Little Men* to become classics for young people of America had they been authored by his daughter under the name of Louisa May Alcox.

But children somehow have a hard time believing all this, for they still wake up on a farm and imagine that they hear, being unmistakably enunciated, the series of sounds: *cock-a-doodle-doo.* The feathered bipeds and the savage little humans refuse to abide by mature man's inhibitory rules.

SIXTEEN

F THIS language of profanity were to be replaced by the language of respectability, one would have to accept all organs of the body as being free from shame. And if the language describing these organs were to be used to personify the individual, or as a metaphor of the personality, there would be some strange-sounding results.

Take, for example, an instance in which a man would be termed *a big prick* or *a perfect prick* in a phallic-worshipping society. What qualities would be expected of such a person?

To deserve the appellation, he should first of all be a well-rounded personality. He should be a firm individual, possibly adamant, highly determined, and have an excellent sense of direction. When he has once set upon a path to pursue, he should be unbending, inflexible, unable and unwilling to be dissuaded from his proper pursuit.

But perfection would require even more remarkable qualities. The individual personifying the organ should be able to retreat unto himself almost at will, shrivelling to a shell when there is neither need nor desire for socialization, and upon such retreat, never losing confidence that he can regain the full stature of his former self.

For he must be a man of stature, *the perfect prick,* and in such a society he would be one who makes contact with other human beings, enjoys such contacts, and imparts pleasures to the others as a result thereof. Although gregarious, however, *the perfect prick* would never impose himself unwanted on another because of search for such contact.

Rising to every occasion, our *perfect prick* enjoys the feeling of power he possesses, but is never compulsive about the use of such power. He does not contend that the power is the end-product in itself, but rather only a means to an end.

In the pro-phallic society, this much-admired individual might have a remarkable degree of self-control, and would exercise this quality particularly during social contacts with another, which he would terminate at a mutually agreeable moment.

Among his other qualities, this individual must have a fine sense of rhythm which he employs in profoundly penetrating movements.

Thus would language reflect the culture in a society that loved the human body; and, if language reflected the culture, the use of such linguistic forms would determine the continuation of such a probiological culture.

4 *Sticks and Stones Will Break My Bones*

SEVENTEEN

O FREQUENTLY are the forbidden words used as personal insults that this characteristic demands some special attention. We have already noted that the organs of the body are appropriated for this purpose, when one calls a person *a prick, an ass, a shmuck,* or *a pendejo.*

In his anger, man seeks terms to express frustration. He resorts to forbidden words because they are inherently stronger in their pejorative character by virtue of their being proscribed. He calls upon ethnic origin,[1] lunacy, and doubtful parentage for the strengthening of this aspect of his vocabulary. He searches for that which is most defamatory, and finds that it inheres in the very nature of disrespectability.[2]

Of the most common pejoratives, other than those that we have already examined, two are somewhat sexual in origin: *son-of-a-bitch* and *bastard*. *The son-of-a-bitch*, frequently used in the abbreviated form of *s.o.b.* or *son-of-a-bee*, does not seem to have acquired mobility upward on the social scale by the substitution of initials for fuller words. Efforts to soften *son-of-a-bitch* in the manner of turning *for Christ's sake* into *for crying out loud* would be expected, and have indeed been made. Such a form as *son-of-a-biscuit* has never caught on, although *son-of-a-gun* is a widely used and rather acceptable substitute.

The bitch, by definition, is the female of the canine and other infrahuman species. In slang, it refers to a woman of socially unacceptable (hence, low) moral standards.[3]

As a word of insult, *bitch* simply describes a person who, in the eyes of the speaker, is nefarious or has done something contemptible. Just as the fluidity of slang permits a woman to be *a prick*, the latter losing its prescribed gender, so it permits a man to be *a bitch*. *He done me dirt*, which makes him *a bitch*.

However, when used in the strictly sexual sense, *the bitch* is less defamatory, and describes only the female, suggesting the combination of sexual desirability and moral undesirability. In one sense, it is complimentary, in the other quite the opposite, but the two meanings that fuse into one word are not mutually exclusive. If anything, they are complementary.

I have a date with a nice bitch, a young man would say, but this is not a date with a girl that he would find proper to marry. Thus are sex and love divorced, and puritanism triumphs in a world of sinners and saints.

When *son-of-a-bitch* is used, it implies contempt more strongly than the lone *bitch.* It loses all literal significance. The reflection on the mother as being of low moral character is entirely lost, except that the powerful kinship drive in a mother-worshipping culture may not only be at the origin of this phrase but may account foɪ the strong reaction of the listener who flares forth in anger when he is addressed by such a term.

How completely apart are the literal and figurative meanings might be seen by the common experience of a man, in anger, calling his brother a *son-of-a-bitch;* or, even more ironical, a mother calling her son by that appellation.

The separation of figurative from literal meaning is completed when *bitch* is used as a pejorative for a male, and *son-of-a-bitch* for a female.

Similar in tone and related to sexuality only in its original meaning is the word *bastard.* Literally, of course, *the bastard* is the illegitimate child, the offspring of illicit sexual relations. Euphemistically, the bastard has been called *the child of love;* in polite society, it is *the child born out of wedlock.*

The generally hostile attitude prevailing against the illegitimate child, whose freedom from culpability in a situation is unquestionable, has often been noted. However, it has a long history relevant to kinship relations in Western society, the primogeniture laws, and Judeo-Christian domination of the marital institution, even in a highly urbanized and essentially secular society.

In ordinary slang, *bastard* is entirely unrelated to the status of birth without benefit of a previous marriage ceremony between one's parents. It is simply a dirty name to call someone. Names will never hurt me, the children are taught to sing in taunting (and even name-calling) manner, but let an adult be called *a son-of-a-bitch bastard* and the little ditty is quickly forgotten.

Sometimes, it seems that these pejoratives have a cathartic function. There is a release of tension by oral violence, and if this does not in its turn incite further tension leading to physical violence, the release may serve beneficially for the user of the insulting term.

Taken directly from the arsenal of sexuality is another and somewhat stronger pejorative, *cocksucker*. Literally, the meaning is self-evident; it could not be described in a single, more accurate and more specific term. That *the cock* refers to the penis, and not to the rooster, is apparent. The word is hence used to describe anyone indulging in fellatio as the so-called passive or recipient party; that is, utilizing one's mouth in oral-genital (mouth-penis) contact. Technically, the term *fellator* is generally used; sometimes a differentiation by sex is made, and the feminine form, *fellatrix,* is given.

H. N. Cary, who writes the term as two words, adds: "Said of either sex." [4]

In a slang dictionary as outspoken as that of Berrey and Van den Bark,[5] a compendium which includes phrases like *fuck around* and *shit-out-of-luck* spelled out without benefit of asterisks, *cocksucker* is prominently absent. The only suggestion of its existence is found in *C-sucker*,[6] a term which the writer has never heard and which may not even exist. It is possible that the authors of the dictionary, in omitting this word, were tacitly implying that it is the most prohibited in the English language.

Any reprobate, any contemptible person, anyone who is to be insulted or defamed, anyone crossing one's path: he (or she) is *a cocksucker*. A man addicted to the use of this word may find it handy thirty or forty times during an evening of conversation. A driver who makes a short stop is *a cocksucker* (that is, if you are behind him); a waiter who spills a little water on your suit, or who brings soup that is not sufficiently warm, is likewise placed in this category; and the name is applied with complete equanimity to the telephone operator who cannot get the right number—but please hang up the receiver before you mutter to yourself this descriptive word about her.

So commonplace is the term that I sat in an automobile with a group of men and heard the word used 161 times during a ride that took less than an hour to complete. By spreading its use in indiscriminate fashion, the defamatory character is of course diluted, yet not sufficiently to deprive it of its anger-inciting qualities when the term is applied to the listener.

It is of interest that, writing on the subject of homosexuality, Cory took note of the dual use of the word *cocksucker*, as both a synonym for fellator and as a general description of one to whom a person is hostile.[7] However, because he was confined within the matrix of homosexuality, Cory saw this duality as being antihomosexual rather than antisexual.

In the puritanical manner that Harper[8] finds characteristic of homosexuals, Cory refers to the word with dashes between the first and last letters: *c— —r* is a printer's convention reminiscent of the asterisks with which literature once abounded.

Aside from his very narrow appropriation of fellatio as a homosexual practice, to which many millions of men and women will take indignant exception, Cory failed entirely to correlate this duality with similar and even stronger terms of defamation applying to all phases of sex. He saw the word being used both to describe homosexuality and other hostility:

> The making of a slang synonym for almost anything or anyone nefarious, with no regard to his sexual inclination, of the term *c— —r* (*sic!*), is comparable only to the hatred expressed by our society against *out-of-wedlock children*, who in addition to being characterized as *illegitimate*, are called *bastards*. Like *c— —r*, the word *bastard* is used to describe anyone on whom contempt is heaped. In this way, an insulting connotation is implied in a word which, in its literal meaning, should merely describe the status or activity of a person.[9]

Quite clearly, Cory was stumbling on a conceptualization of the duality without ambiguity of dirty words, but was unable, because of his narrow interests and his confining frame of reference, to relate the concept to all tabooed words involved in tabooed biological activities.

5 *Euphemist, What's the Good Word?*

EIGHTEEN

I F, AS Burke[1] has stated, slang was invented as an antidote to grammar, then euphemism, I would add, was in many instances invented as an antidote to slang.

Masturbation is a particularly interesting example not only of this process but of its very opposite as well. Masturbation is not entirely free from description by proscribed language, which follows the pattern already seen for defecation and micturition as well as for parts of the body.

Of all technical terms of a sexual nature, the word *masturbation* is probably one of the best known and most universally used. It can be found in medical books; yet, unlike most technical terminology, it is known to the public and can be used in modern parlor conversation. It is understood by young people at a tender age; almost as soon as they learn the process do they learn the word that describes it.

A synonym for masturbation, *onanism,* is relatively little known and hardly used outside of a few texts.

Nevertheless, *masturbation* has its euphemistic circumlocutious synonyms and its forbidden counterparts. Of the former, *to play with himself* (or *herself*) is probably the most widely used, and one is very careful to differentiate this from a closely related expression: *to play by himself.* Thus, a mother would advise her little boy to go off and *play by himself,* but not *with himself,* although he might find it possible to combine the two activities into a single process.

If the language of sexuality abounds with euphemisms, which express the thought while cushioning its harshness, it likewise is abundant in the very opposite of euphemisms. These would be words and phrases which express a thought in a manner that increases the hostility or harshness, and for this I had thought of coining the word *cacophemisms,* until I learned that Read[2] had suggested it many years ago, together with an alternate choice, the coined synonym *dysphemisms.*

This last word I have also found in a work by the French writer Carnoy, who so cogently stated: "Dysphemism is a stimulant, whereas euphemism is a sedative." [3] It is the concept that is important, and either word being satisfactory, it is cacophemism that will be used here.

Masturbation is described with two particularly nefarious cacophemisms, *the solitary sin* and *self-abuse*. By their use, a person describes the masturbatory act and simultaneously characterizes it and condemns it. More than that, he makes the value judgment synonymous with the act itself.

It was natural for D. H. Lawrence who, from the vantage-point of a generation later, we can now see as more puritan than prurient, to speak of "the act of self-abuse" for he was quite unfriendly to masturbation:

> Instead of being a comparatively pure and harmless vice, masturbation is certainly the most dangerous sexual vice that a society can be afflicted with, in the long run.[4]

Or again, comparing masturbation with sexuality between two individuals, he finds that in the former

> there is nothing but loss. There is no reciprocity. There is merely the spending away of a certain force, but no return. The body remains, in a sense, a corpse, after the act of self-abuse.[4]

Turning from the euphemisms and cacophemisms, we find, as would be expected, that masturbation has its slang expressions, two of which are frequently employed: *to jerk off* (with slight variation, *to jack off*), and *to pull off*. The latter is sometimes used in its literal and accepted meaning: *he pulled off the sweater*, and no confusion would result. Alone, however, ending the sentence at the word *off*, the meaning is clear.

Both of these words represent a degree of profanity that is rather mild. They are dirty words, but they are not very dirty; they are simply slightly soiled. On a continuum from respectability to disrespectability, they are located at a point almost as far from *masturbation* as they are from *shit*.

One might conjecture on the possibility that both of these terms originated with an unconscious castration wish, at least when used by the male and when concerning the male process. The phrases suggest that something is attached, and by a pulling or jerking motion, the attached piece might become detached. The word *off* suggests disassociation from, as when one takes something *off* the table. However, this genetic derivation of the phrase is only a suggestion, and is difficult to verify.

Whatever the origin, the word *jerk* certainly expresses a hostile social attitude, when used in a slang that seems to be of rather recent vintage. A person is called *a jerk* to indicate that he is a fool, that he allows another to get the better of him. A person is told *to stop jerking around* to express a desire that he should stop wasting time and doing useless things.

Thus, language expresses its antagonism to the masturbatory process by using euphemisms to avoid direct mention of the phenomenon, by using cacophemisms to express the hostility as something built into the linguistic structure, and by appropriating the slang for other hostile expressions in a manner similar to that done for excretory acts and products.

NINETEEN

MASTURBATION is usually (although not always) performed alone; hence the cacophemism, *the solitary sin*. It has in common with involuntary nocturnal emission the absence of a sex partner, save in fantasy or dream life. Both are surrounded by an aura of guilt, shame, and sin. This, however, is not true of another process, menstruation. Just the opposite, in fact: it is a reward for not having sinned, or for having done so with due care and prudence.

Menstruation is surrounded in all lands by a vast folklore, mythology, and superstition. The language of menstruation, particularly in the U.S.A., and the influence of class and ethnic origin on the language, has been studied and summarized by Joffe.[5] In general, the terminology reflects the concept that the process is dirty, but not sinful. Hence, there is no obscene language that is borrowed for figurative (and usually negative) purposes.

This is not the case with the involuntary emission, often called, in technical literature, *a nocturnal emission.* The latter phrase expresses the fact that the process usually takes place at night, and thus it suggests, if only by implication, that it is during the sleeping period. Hence, the involuntary nature of the act differentiates it from masturbation.

Curiously enough, the forbidden expression for nocturnal emission, *the wet dream,* is more accurate, even if it has a connotation of dirtiness that results from its being prohibited. The accuracy is derived from the literal meaning: there is a dream, there is wetness, and the two are related in a cause-and-effect sequence.

One of the most interesting examples of the use of cacophemism in the language of sexuality is found in technical and scientific literature, when the involuntary emission is termed *a nocturnal pollution.*

Pollution is, of course, the act of soiling, of rendering dirty.

Even a writer as scientific as Malinowski, who exhibited not only a friendly attitude toward sexual expression but a remarkable grasp of the relationship between linguistics and culture, could unconsciously fall into the error of the caco-phemism:

> The new manhood influences above all the boy's sexual outlook. Mentally he is ready for knowledge, physiologi-cally ready for applying it in life. Usually he receives his first lessons in sex at this time, and in some form or other starts sexual activities, not so often, probably, in the nor-mal, regular manner, but frequently through masturba-tion or nocturnal pollutions.[6]

It may be argued that soiling does take place; hence there is pollution. Why deny it or be defensive about it? My argu-ment is not a denial of the soiling, although it is doubtful if this is true of primitive groups, such as Malinowski was de-scribing. Soiling only occurs when one is neatly tucked away for the night, as between two sheets; dirtiness and pollution are culturally-defined phenomena.

However, the question in the cacophemism is not whether there is soiling. It is that the speaker extracts one character-istic or quality and reifies it by making it synonymous with the entire experience. Why not call it *nocturnal ecstasy, noc-turnal tension relief,* or *nocturnal fantasy*? All of these would be as accurate as *nocturnal pollution.* But this is not done. The language reflects the cultural attitudes, and thereupon reinforces them.

6

Luv is a Three-Letter Word

TWENTY

HE ADOLESCENT, growing in his aware-
ness of sexuality, is constantly developing and creating the
language of prohibited terminology. His vocabulary, although satisfactorily expressive, is unceasingly expanding. The
abundance of neologisms imparts a feeling, to the youthful
males who create and perpetuate them, of ribaldry, vitality,
and strength of a masculine character.

Thus, a sense of peer-group identification is imparted to
the youth who can talk sex with a large arsenal of words that

are admired precisely because they are proscribed. In his terminology he betrays simultaneously his desire for the female body and his contempt for all those whom he can desire: the omnipresent ambivalence that Albert Ellis[1] has so aptly termed the "American sexual tragedy."

It is to be expected that the erogenous zone of female anatomy most apparent to the onlooker should be honored with the most abundant vocabulary. The vagina may be dreamed about, lusted after, and even talked of, but the girl walking down the street does not make a display of that area of the body, as she does with her breasts.

Standing on the corner, watching the parade, young men spend hours admiring, describing, passing judgment on the girls who walk by, and much of their descriptive conversation centers around the breasts.

Thus, the passing girl has *teats* (or *tits*), also known as *TNT,* the explosive initials standing for *two nifty teats.* This, the most common word for breasts, is one of contempt, as it makes the woman synonymous with a lower animal in a highly anthropocentric society.

Although the breasts are called *nuts* or *balls,* the context prevents any confusion with the much wider usage of these names for testicles.

Because of the area of the body and the general shape, the girl is said to have *lungs,* while in a more picturesque vein one finds the word *headlights.*

Bosom spelled backwards gives the girl *mosob,* while the general shape gives her *pellets, knobs, balloons, bumps,* and *molehills.*

From the language of fruit, one obtains *lemons, oranges, grapefruits,* and even *watermelons,* although more frequently just plain *melons,* not to overlook *apples,* the variety of which is not specified.

In addition, and by no means exhausting the list, there are *boobs, racks, tonsils, bags, plates, growths, warts,* and one should not omit the very utilitarian *milkers, milk bottles,* and *pumps.*

Unlike other parts of the vocabulary of erotica, these words are only rarely used, whether in slang or in accepted vocabulary, in a derogatory manner. This may be because they are purely descriptive, albeit there is an element of exaggeration in analogic derivation when the breasts are equated with watermelons.

The descriptive terminology for breasts is comparable to that of the penis being called *the pipe,* the hymen termed *the cherry,* or the pubic hair described as *the bush.* All these words are prohibited, they are not nice to use, but they are borrowed from accepted descriptive language and serve functionally to communicate a physical image.

In these instances, the word first existed as symbol of a thing, and the thing was nonerotic; however, the thing symbolized, in form, shape, and perhaps size, a second object, this time erotic, and the word was thereupon appropriated for a new purpose. Having come into the language as accepted terminology, it usually does not come to be used in a defamatory manner about nonbiological concepts.

The abundance of words for breasts, of which the above is but a minute sampling, is an index of the intense interest in the anatomy of the female on the part of the most imaginative and creative slang-using groups, and of the need for masculine identification with peer groups among those who display toward the breast the ambivalence of shame and want, fear and desire, guilt and lust.[2]

TWENTY-ONE

ROFANITY cannot, of course, be studied without focusing attention on the sexual act. The word *profane* itself literally means *temporal, unholy, lacking sanctity*; it means *worldly* as distinct from *otherworldly*. To be profane is *to be godless*, to treat holy things in an irreverent manner.

Thus, to say the Lord's name in an unholy manner was profane; hence, profanity included such phrases as *go to hell* or *Jumping Jesus!* But words change their meanings as language evolves, and as religious institutions no longer play the role in the life of modern man that they once did, profanity encompasses a wider, a more secular field, taking in the entire scope of forbidden words, and particularly those that are associated with the biological functions of excretion and sex, and the organs that perform them.

The euphemisms that are used to describe sexual activity often state the opposite of what is intended. A man is said *to sleep around* with many women, when the one thing he is probably not doing with the women is going to sleep. We say that *he sleeps with her,* to denote an incident that may have occurred over a duration of five or ten minutes, in the back seat of an automobile or elsewhere under conditions in which sleep would be well-nigh impossible.

Thus, *to sleep with* and *to sleep around* may have many implications, but one thing they do not mean, and that is *to sleep.*

A man is said *to be making love to her,* or they are said *to have made love together,* to express performance of a sexual act, although there may be no question of love, and no pretense of affirmation of affection. Although *love* is here used to avoid the clumsy or the forbidden, because it is so employed it undergoes a change of character. Thus, in their study of the folklore and language of the Ozarks, Randolph and Wilson noted: "Even the word *love* is considered more or less indecent, and mountain people seldom use it in its ordinary sense, but nearly always with some degrading or jocular connotation...." [3]

Not quite so topsy-turvy is the expression: *to have an*

affair. We say of a man that *he had many affairs,* thus imparting to a word which originally referred to businesslike ventures some activities somewhat less businesslike in character.

These three euphemisms, and many others, are called into play because the modern American or Englishman just has no way of expressing the fact of sexual intercourse without clumsy and technical terms, on the one hand, or profanity, on the other.

To say of two people that *they copulated,* that *they cohabited,* or that *they had sexual relations* is just not good conversational English, does not come naturally, and is stilted, while to say that *they screwed* or *fucked* is shocking.

The euphemisms are necessary because the thought of sex is itself not shocking, but only the sounds; so that if one might only express the same thought, while not quite saying it, the objections would be overcome.

The biological terms, the euphemisms, and the circumlocutions being inadequate, the language must develop simple words that express the process with a minimum of ambiguity.

These words, although as a group proscribed, have a hierarchy of prohibition. To take the three most frequently encountered, one can set them forth in order of diminishing acceptability: *to lay* (or its variation, *to get laid*), *to screw,* and *to fuck.*

This quality of respectability is in inverse ratio to the degree with which the words are used in nonsexual slang and the strength of the derogatory, defamatory, or pejorative character implicit in such usage.

Just as *P* or *pea* is never employed in the nonbiological

argot, *piss* only in mild phrases and in one instance actually in a favorable connotation, and *shit* in stronger expressions, so a parallelism can be drawn with these three sexual terms.

The failure to find *lay* or *laid* in figurative slang is thus inherent in the slang, and is not to be traced to the existence of the word as a verb in proper English.

Passing on to *screw,* this word (like *balls*) has its accepted meaning. As a noun, *a screw* is an article of hardware, a nail-like metallic piece with spiral formations that permit one to drive into a receptacle by a turning or twisting motion. The verb *to screw* would be the act of turning with a twisting motion; but as a verb, it is little used in this manner, because of the embarrassing hint of copulatory action. The literal definition, however, has enough of a suggestion of the movements of penis into vagina to enable one to trace the etiology of this slang. The analogy is interesting. It suggests passivity and resistance by the female; struggle to enter by the male.

Sex is something, of course, that a nice girl is not supposed to like, but submits to with reluctance because the male has the devil in his flesh. By appropriating the verb *screw* for sexual description, a society perpetuates this concept, and at the same time permits the conquering warrior male to retain an image of himself as having forced himself upon the reluctant female. The language is a reflection of a society that abhors sex while idolizing the male who obtains it and denouncing the female who offers it.

In the history of English-language slang, respectable slang, printable in the most proper books, that omit even such suggestions as *s**t,* the word *screw* is always found, but sel-

dom with mention of its sexual meaning. Among many defini-
tions, *a screw* is a prison guard[4] in the language of the underworld and of the prisoner; and *a screw* is also a teacher who
gives particularly difficult examinations.[5]

The verb *to screw* means *to extort*,[6] a colloquialism that
some lexicographers today accept as having passed into the
confines of complete propriety. However, in all these instances, *screw* is somewhat negative, mildly pejorative.

In modern-day slang, the teacher is no longer called *a
screw* when his examinations prove difficult. There are many
colloquialisms much more expressive, albeit less specifically
descriptive of his penchant for making the tests so tough.
However, out of earshot, the student is likely to use the word,
although not in the manner of some decades ago; he will
express his contempt by saying, to himself or to a fellow-
student, that *the teacher can go screw himself for all he cares.*

Probably derived from the slang equivalent for extort,
there is the expression: *to put the screws on someone,* meaning to apply extreme pressure to compel a given course of
action. Particularly in the passive form (*they put the screws
on me*), but even in the active one, there is here an expression
of unpleasant pressure, of compulsion, of the application of
force to have an act performed unwillingly and involuntarily.

The prison guard continues to receive the appellation of
screw, while many other slang usages of this word have made
their way into the language, for neologistic fluidity is more
characteristic of slang than of other forms of verbal or written
communication.

A person is *screwy* if he is *off the beam,* if he is not entirely in possession of his mental faculties, if he is on the wrong track. Not only might he be *screwy,* but his ideas can be *screwy,* or his plans.

Like *nuts, screwy* has very wide latitude, ranging from mildly foolish to literally insane, from describing one who is reasoning poorly in a specific instance to another who is completely devoid of reasoning power. As a synonym for insane, it has fallen into disrepute, for the same reason that this has happened to *nuts.*

An unusual opportunity to determine whether the figurative use of the sexual slang is a reflection (as well as a reinforcement) of the antisexual attitudes of our culture is found in an examination of the differences between the word *screw* in England and in America.

In England, *screw* is little used in its sexual connotation. It is employed widely in slang, not only for the *prison guard,* for unhappy pressure (*putting the screws on him*), and other idiomatic expressions, but has a very favorable slang meaning as well, namely *a salary.*

Despite the abundance of American servicemen who went to England during World War II, and who certainly used obscene language with utter abandon, the sexual meaning of the word *screw* is still almost unknown to large numbers of people in that country, and the favorable slang meaning equally unknown on the western side of the Atlantic. This would seem to indicate that, although it is possible for the same slang word to be used in both positive and negative qualifying phrases, this does not occur when the word has sexual significance.

The difference between the manner in which the word is used in the two countries gives rise to many embarrassing situations. "An English typist may be heard to say, 'My employer gives me a nice little *screw* every week,'" writes Weber.[7] "This sentence would have an extremely vulgar meaning in America, and English people should guard against using the word in this slang sense."

Elliot tells of an incident that he calls "an Anglo-American *faux-pas*":

> "Does the man on this job get a good *screw?*" I asked. The engineer looked a bit startled and then he and Croft burst out laughing. This customary and innocent sounding phrase to British ears means something quite different, and not very respectable, on the other side, as also does the remark, "I am all knocked up." Say this in the presence of a woman and you'll find yourself right in Dutch.[8]

A figurative meaning of the word *screw* is in the characterization of a person as *a screwball*. This is mildly defamatory, somewhat insulting, but more likely expresses oddness, impracticality, foolhardiness, nonconformity, usually with an unacceptable connotation, but possibly in a fond and eye-winking manner, much as one would say that someone is *a bohemian*. There is no lack of intelligence, no flight from sanity, here expressed.

The suggestion of insanity is stated, however, when one says of a person that he has *a screw loose*; in other words, that the components of the brain which, in the ordinarily intelligent human being are held together by screws and other hardware, have come apart. They are no longer in normal functional relationship to each other.

The use of these words in a trichotomous manner (hardware, sexual slang, nonsexual slang) is expressed in a story told of a young man who had recently been graduated from a journalism school and had obtained a job on a small-town newspaper. There was no division by specialization into reporters, rewrite men, and headline writers; the neophyte had to do the entire job himself.

Although proficient in gathering information and writing the story, the youthful journalist, to the dismay of his editor, wrote heads that were long, wordy, and cumbersome. One day, the editor called him aside and gave him a lecture on the use of short, pithy terms in heads: abbreviations, slang, neologisms, colloquialisms, whatever might be required to express the meaning in a small and restricted number of printer's characters.

The following day the young journalist learned that a man had escaped from a mental institution, run amok, terrorized a neighboring town, and raped a woman. In all its flavorful detail, the reporter zestfully wrote his story, and after pondering over it with some satisfaction, sent it to press with the headline:

NUT BOLTS AND SCREWS

One of the most common uses of *screw* is in the phrase *screwed up*. This can refer either to a person, a place, or a situation. One would say that *the job got all screwed up,* or that *the student screwed up the experiment in the laboratory,* or that the man is confused, neurotic, hence *screwed up.*

Like many other unofficial expressions, *screwed up* gives latitude that is best understood in its full context. It can be mixed up, disarranged, gone astray or gone awry, helter-skelter, in a bad condition. The individual who is *screwed up* may be confused, either generally or with regard to a particular issue; or he may be quite anxiety-ridden, disturbed, neurotic; or perhaps only on the wrong track.

But *a person gets screwed* when he gets the short end of the stick, when someone betrays him. One says that he worked very hard when his employer needed him, only to be fired in the slow season: *his boss screwed him,* or *he got a screwing.* Or the same thing would be said of a girl, and it is difficult to imagine any ambiguity.

Sometimes these words are given picturesque modifiers that soon become repeated until they are clichés of the shadow language, for the users of tabooed terminology favor both the cliché and the neologism; they sponsor the former by the frequency with which they call upon the same words and phrases, and the latter by the manner in which they work obscenities into unexpected constructions, uninhibited by the boundaries of formal rules.

An adjectival modifier that embellishes the word *screwing* is found in the phrase *a royal screwing,* meaning a betrayal, a stab in the back, not of an ordinary type, but more so.

One would say *he got a royal screwing,* not to signify some sexual relationship with a queen, a princess, or some lesser member of the reigning family, but rather to signify that *someone did him in,* that *someone did him dirt.*

Ambiguity between the biological and nonbiological is deliberately employed in one area of American culture, namely the dirty joke. A considerable part of off-color humor is probably centered around this type of double meaning, of which one example will be cited here.

Mr. Brown and Mr. Green were partners in a thriving business. They had a private plane, which Mr. Brown would pilot, and when they went on a business trip, each one took his secretary along with him. On one such trip, Mr. Brown suddenly yelled to his partner, "Jack, quick, the plane's on fire, put on your parachute, we gotta jump."

"What about the girls?" Green demanded.

"Screw the girls," came the quick retort, to which Green replied:

"You think we got time?"

The figurative meaning of *screw* can be not merely non-sexual in character, but actually antisexual. Just as a man who will not copulate with his girl friend because it is not nice might be called by his friends, of all things, *a big prick*— the one thing he literally has not been—so a girl who is frigid and has deep-going sexual phobias might be referred to by her friends as *all screwed up*—the one thing she literally is not.

TWENTY-TWO

IN THE entire language of proscribed words, from slang to profanity, from the mildly unclean to the utterly obscene, including terms relating to concealed parts of the body, to excretion and excrement as well as to sexuality, one word reigns supreme, unchallenged in its preeminence. It sits upon a throne, an absolute monarch, unafraid of any princely offspring still unborn, and by its subjects it is hated, feared, revered and loved, known by all and recognized by none.

When one refers to *a four-letter word,* all other words of four letters fade from the language; one does not think of *have* or *five,* of *love* or *bite.* When someone puts out a cook book entitled *Food is a Four Letter Word,* the title is not only titillatingly pornographic, but it is entirely untrue.[9] *Food* is not *a four-letter word;* there is only one *four-letter word* in the English language.

When a Harvard lyricist wanted to ridicule the arch-enemy of his beloved institution, he wrote: *Yale is a four-letter word,* whereupon his song was censored.[10] Count the letters in the name *Yale,* and they come to four, but the monarch rules supreme: there is one king and only one, and *Yale* is not *a four-letter word.*

When one sees a word written as *f* followed by a dash or some asterisks, as *f—* or *f***,* one need not wonder whether the term refers to *fair* or *foul,* to *fame* or *folly,* to *fathead* or *fatuousness.* The monarch reigns over the language.

No other word of the English language could be so readily understood with so little explication, and yet, poor *fuck,* it is not even permitted to gain access to our greatest and most complete lexicographical efforts.

So overwhelming is the effect of this sound on Americans that, when they learn a foreign language which contains a formation homonymous with it, as the French *le phoque,* they block it out, they cannot learn to say it, they cannot recall it.

It would seem that, devoid of all linguistic association, and placed in the framework of another tongue, the sound formations themselves become taboo-linked. They are sounds that can be enunciated only as one fulfills one's role as an actor in an assigned and accepted manner: the American boy in boy's company, the men and women in a sophisticated group. The same sounds, stripped of all possible forbidden connotations, are unutterable when one's role is changed to that of student.

When one refers to *an Anglo-Saxon monosyllable,* no one thinks of *go* or *big,* of *bread* or *knife.* There is only one such *Anglo-Saxonism,* although there is some dispute as to whether it did in fact derive from Old English, Partridge giving credit to Greek, Latin, and French ancestries, with a Teutonic root for the medial *c.*[11] In a magnificent five-volume study entitled *Sexual Vocabulary,* Cary mentions that the etymology has apparently never been traced, and then proceeds to suggest that it is onomatopoeic![12]

Is England, already deprived of so much of her Empire, to lose the battle for control of its most famous Anglo-Saxon monosyllable? Partridge, spelling the word alternately with one asterisk and two on the very same page, says that it is probably one of the sadistic group of words for man's part in copulation. It may have been derived, he writes, from an old word meaning *to strike,* or might even come from the Sanskrit, while Buck relates it to *fyke* and *fike* (move restlessly or *fidget*), and finds evidence of John le Fucker in the thirteenth century.[13]

That a simple, universally understood, short and pithy term is needed to express copulation is apparent, and every language has such a word, although only a few peoples have been so frightened by it that they have relegated it to the realm of the oft-mentioned unmentionables.

However, if our thesis has any validity, then one could predict that a study of the nonsexual usages of the word *fuck* and expressions and phrases in which it is found would display hostile attitudes toward people, places, things, situations, and processes. This is indeed the case.

Like *balls* and *shit,* the word *fuck* by itself, usually followed by an exclamation point if proper grammatical usage is to be upheld, is an expletive. It expresses dismay, but the situation in which it is uttered is not necessarily more distressing than an analogous one in which a slightly weaker dirty word is called into play.

Despite the strong survival qualities of the tabooed words, some do drop out of earshot. Farmer[14] cites *fucker,* as both a term of endearment and derision. My own studies would indicate that the word is hardly in use today, but other derivatives are anything but obsolete.

When preceded by the word *mother,* a combination with *fucker* is made that is unique in its ability to incite aggressive anger even among people who have developed an armor of defense against the insults derived from obscenity. Perhaps mankind's overwhelming fear of incest is challenged when the word *mother-fucker* is heard; or perhaps the image of the mother as pure and inviolate is damaged when the tabooed sounds are spoken. Although an example of a term that is both sexually descriptive and figuratively insulting, *mother-fucker* seems to touch off such a sensitive area, even in the speaker and insulter, that it has not passed into the general language of taboos that are violated at the rate of several per minute.

Much more frequently utilized, for example, is *fucked up*. Like *screwed up*, the expression means disarrayed, mixed up, in a bad shape, handled badly, improperly, ineptly. One says that *the job got all fucked up*, that *the clerk in the army fucked up the discharge papers*, or that *the lawyer fucked up things, but good, in preparing the case*.

In this last instance, the word *good* is especially important, because it communicates that the lawyer did an exceptionally *bad* job. It is possible to use *good* in the sense of meaning bad, because it literally means *to a very considerable extent* as a modifier of the slang.

The adverbial modifier *up* is itself a curious phenomenon; first, because one does not literally *fuck up*, but *down*; and second, because *up* is usually synonymous with goodness, with things being on a high level, as *things are looking up*.

Just as *a person got screwed* or *got a screwing* when he was maltreated or betrayed, so it is said of him (or her) that *he got fucked* or *got a fucking*, the former being preferred (the preference is only linguistic, however).

To waste time, to loaf or idle, is *to fuck around* or, less frequently, *to fuck the dog*, while to cheat or to defraud someone is *to fuck your way out of a situation*.

To make the word somewhat more palatable, *fucked up* is occasionally changed to *fouled up*, while *oh fuck* is changed to *oh fudge*, an alteration even more repugnant to the sophisticated than the sweetly substitutive *sugar* for *shit*.

TWENTY-THREE

IN A LONG phrase that attained considerable popularity during the Second World War in the armed forces of the United States, it would be said: *situation normal all fucked up*. In this phrase, *fucked* is not only used to denote badly handled, but the word *normal* makes the negative character stronger by imposing a value judgment on the Army or Navy. Later, the initials *snafu* (or *snafud*) came to be used and, as in all other instances, required an antecedent which was readily available: *situation normal all fouled up*.

As an adjectival modifier, *fuckin* (or *fucking, fucken,* or *fuckin'*) became in recent years one of the most abundantly uttered sounds in the English language. While frequently seen in the literature as *fucking,* this writer prefers the more phonetically exact version *fuckin.* In all-male circles, and in the armed services, the number of times in which the word could be worked into a conversation would be the criterion by which one would judge the masculinity, the sophistication, or the freedom from taboos, of a speaker.

While it indiscriminately modifies almost every word, and expresses almost anything and hence almost nothing, the general tone of its use is indubitably derogatory. *The fuckin driver can't drive, the fuckin teacher* is *no fuckin good,* who said we should come to *this fuckin bar* where *the beer is fuckin warm* and we have to wait for *fuckin service* from *the fuckin waitress.*

Dean Inge, commenting on the word *bloody,* said that it had no ponderable meaning, but was a sort of notice that a noun was coming.[15] How true of *fuckin,* except that we can add: or another adjective. Farmer, in his work of the late nineteenth century, preferred the *ing* spelling, and said it was a qualification of extreme contumely.[16]

Occasionally, the universality of the word will lead to its being used in a neutral or even in a slightly laudatory context: it is conceivable that one can say of another that he has been *a fuckin good friend.* This may be due to the generally watered-down tone resulting from frequency of use, as Graves has suggested, or it may be an evocation of the superlative character of a friendship that is strong enough to permit being described in such intimate terms. In any case, it can have affectionate, warm and positive feelings only when modifying an adjective, never a noun. *This is a fuckin good meal* means the very opposite of *what a fuckin meal.*

However, the negative nature of the figurative uses of the word *fuck* is most strongly emphasized in the expressions *fuck you* and *go fuck yourself,* which might be considered synonymous with *drop dead,* and like the latter, are not meant for literal interpretation.

Whatever the exact meaning in the expression *go fuck yourself,* it is a hostile order, a rejection, a command to go off and be unhappy and to do something unpleasant and unrewarding to yourself.

In pointing out the absurdity of ordering someone to go away and obtain the greatest pleasure known to man because we want to punish him for his transgressions, Albert Ellis suggests that it would be more appropriate to give the command: *go unfuck yourself.*[17]

In a previous section, we mentioned the expression: *I don't give a shit,* as being synonymous with *I just don't care a hoot.* The same expression is used with the word *fuck: I don't give a fuck.*

The parent of both of these expressions is probably *I don't give a damn* coming from the slang expression for *tinker's damn* (or *dam*) which was synonymous with *worthless.* In the two modern versions, the same expressions are used, with the epitome of worthlessness being found in the product of excretion and the act of sexuality.

Whatever the context, whatever the expression, *fuck* is

surrounded with defamatory and derogatory connotations in its nonsexual usage. From what is known about all other words pertaining to excretion and sexuality, it could hardly be otherwise.

7

Linguistics: Erotica and Curiosa

HE LANGUAGE of forbidden words gives rise to unlikely and unusual, in fact almost impossible, syntactical structures, some of which are difficult to account for by the ordinary rules that govern the English tongue, others unique if not to obscenities then at least to slang.

For example, authors have long noted the quaint British custom of inserting the word *bloody* right into the middle of another word. In English, writes Ashley Montagu,[1] "we have affixes and suffixes but no real infixes, although the cockney's *abso-bloody-lutely* or *im-bloody-possible,* which introduces a whole word into the middle of the original to give it greater intensity, is based on the principle." According to Mencken,[2] Joseph Pulitzer is reported to have roared at one of his managing editors that "you are too *indegoddampendent*," and the same managing editor, Foster Coates, is said to have told Pulitzer that he was under no *obligoddamnation* to do something or other.

Still another example is given in a recent novel by Alan Sillitoe:[3] "She squealed out: 'Christ *All-bleedin'-mighty!* Somebody got me that one!' " And John Wain[4] gives an excellent example of how *bloody* can be used, when one of his characters says: "Outside, mister . . . *Out bloody side.*"

From these examples, one can well understand the comment by Julian Franklyn,[5] that "the Cockney puts intrusive syllables into many words, and automatically uses an inter-syllable expletive as though the insertion were an essential part of the word. *Absobloodylutely* is heard almost as often as the simple 'absolutely.' "

In addition to *bloody,* the English use *bleeding* as an insert between two words. The following is a record of English speech made by a New York reporter in England:

> "Blimey," he cried when he saw us. "May I bloody-well be struck dumb blind and bloodywell dead if it isn't me bloody Yank ally. At bloody last you've come back to the only friends you *absobleedinglutely* have got bloodywell left."[6]

Not true infixes, as Montagu states, these linguistic peculiarities were given a new name by Wentworth,[7] who termed them *sandwich words*; Sapir,[8] in fact, describes the infix as a phenomenon "utterly unknown in English."

But *bloody* and *goddam* are not the only sandwich fillings, for it became a not infrequent practice, particularly among the armed forces and in other youthful groups, to use *fuckin* (or modifications thereof) in order to form sandwich words. Some such words are difficult to spell, and this may be the first time that they have been reduced to writing, so that one can only follow the pronunciation, modified by the usual orthography for the various morphemes.

Examples of sandwich words that have been used with some frequency include *irrefuckinsponsible, imfuckinpossible, unfuckinconscious,* and *unfuckinsociable.* In each instance, it is possible that the substitution of an *e* for the *i* following the *k* might more closely approximate the pronunciation.

A neologism foreign not only to the language in which it is employed, but to the entire group of languages to which the tongue is related, may be difficult to formulate orally. Slang requires phonetic ease, and if one stumbles over a word, or has to state it slowly, the word will die before it is born. This may account for a peculiar variation of *disafuckingreeable,* in which the two syllables of the sandwiched section (or the infix) are reversed, and the word is pronounced somewhat more closely resembling *disinfuckagreeable.*

I am reliably informed of a conversation heard in a

British barracks during the recent war. A few soldiers were playing cards, while on the other side of the room the radio was blasting forth, with Axis Sally exhorting and appealing to her listeners in their native tongue. One of the card players yelled to his buddies near the radio: "Turn off the propafuckenganda!" [9]

Aside from these and the previous examples cited by such writers as Weseen,[10] Mencken, Wentworth, and Montagu as being possibly unique word formations in the English tongue, one might here stop to note the generally negative qualities of the words in which the infix is inserted. One utilizes sex to form the filling of a sandwich when the surrounding parts are negative and unappealing.

TWENTY-FIVE

HE SANDWICH word, however, is not the only linguistic peculiarity that crops up in the realm of slang and obscenity, for there may be intrusive syllables sandwiched not into words, but into phrases; and two words may not only become one, but one word, in this manner, may become two.

Frederick Packard,[11] in 1946, coined the word *schizoverbia*, which is a phenomenon occurring when one takes a multiple word and splits it in two, "juggling it around or trimming it up a bit to turn it into a descriptive phrase." Among other examples of schizoverbia cited by Packard are these gems: "Oh shut up you *ragged little muffins!*" and a description of an income tax return as the "most *rigged-up marole*" that had ever been seen.

But it is not only the single word that is split in two; the same thing has long been happening to phrases. Everyone has heard such a phrase as: *Why the hell don't you fix it?* The insert, *the hell,* almost defies syntactical analysis; it is an intrusion into a tight little phrase, splitting it into two parts, and giving added emphasis to the entire sentence.

Technically, the closest term that describes this phenomenon is *tmesis,* defined by Fowler[12] as "the separation of the parts of a compound word by another word inserted between them, as when 'toward us' is written *to usward,* or 'whatsoever things' *what things soever.*" Mario Pei and Frank Gaynor[13] give tmesis a broader definition, calling by this term "the interpolation of a word between the parts of a compound word or expression."

Taking a leaf from Packard and his schizoverbia, it would seem that the most accurate method of describing the intrusion of one or two words into a tight phrase or idiomatic expression would be to call this *schizophrasia,* a phenomenon probably more widespread when obscenities are used than at any other time.

For example, one can insert *the fuck* into the middle of a sentence or phrase, splitting the sequence into two separated personalities, when they would ordinarily be expected to follow one another without interruption. The insertion of these words, that takes place almost invariably in an atmosphere of hostility, seems to emphasize this quality.

Thus, one underlines the hostile and aggressive order in *sit down* by making it *sit the fuck down,* and in the same way *shut up* becomes *shut the fuck up.*

The imperative verbs *sit* and *shut* are, in these instances, intransitive; the sentences are not structurally analogous to *sit the baby down* or *shut the baby up.* The insertion of *the fuck* is not as a direct object, and therefore defies linguistic analysis. Because it is found in a relatively out-group milieu, its use might be a metaphor of a defiant attitude toward society.

Somewhat less hostile, except that it reflects a general air of disgust, is the use of *fuckin* as an inserted word interrupting the usual sequence, in the colloquy: "What time is it?" "It's half past fuckin four."

Schizophrasia, like the sandwich, illustrates that the fluidity of slang is restricted by the internalization of the negative attitude toward all things sexual, so that the words and phrases in question can be formed only if they are on the one hand phonetically pronounceable, and on the other if they are expressive of hostility.

8 *In the Beginning There Was a Seed*

TWENTY-SIX

HE TRAGIC confusion of the society in its attitude toward sex is reflected in the language of ejaculation, also known in evasive but accurately descriptive terminology as *the climax*.

Two words are commonly used for the ejaculatory process: *to come* and *to shoot*. The first is pathetically passive and lacking in fervor, a far cry from the French argot for the same act, *jouir*, which literally means to enjoy. And the second, *to shoot?* It has a pleasant association with buds and children that shoot up, but the spasms suggest potential aggression, antagonism, as if one had an enemy, not a partner. This analysis of the word was to some extent substantiated, linguistically, when the writer recently came across another phrase, used in low-economic circles as a synonymous expression for *I came*: namely, *I got my revenge.* It would be difficult to imagine a linguistic device that would express more accurately the aggressive and hostile attitude of a man toward his partner.

Literally, the worst is yet to come.

The fluid that the male ejaculates as the culmination of erotic stimulation is, in proper society, known as *semen,* a word widely understood and used without discomfort in many social groups, in mature and well-educated circles, and in middle- and upper-class socioeconomic strata.

When dried up, the semen is called, in the tabooed language, *crud,* which is probably a corruption of *curd.* The former is occasionally used as a synonym for *shit,* and, as pointed out by Wentworth and Flexner, is found in several derivative and nonbiological meanings to denote things disgusting.[1]

But the key word in this language is one used primarily in lower-economic groups, and among youngsters, particularly in the urbanized areas of the eastern part of the United States, where semen is called *scum* and the condom is known as *the scum bag.*[2]

The dictionary definition of *scum* is well known. Literally, it is waste material that floats at the top of a fluid-containing receptacle. Figuratively, it is refuse, any waste, and particularly anything vile and worthless. *Scum* is the epitome of the low, dirty, evil, and in proper societies is so used to apply to people who are looked upon as degraded. Those who are denigrated and deprecated—they are *scum*. Vile and worthless—*they are the scum of the earth*.

And what would an anthropologist coming from the enlightened peoples of the African bush or from the Australian aborigines say when he learned that the lowest and dirtiest thing on earth was described with the same word that is used for semen? Aside from his utter disbelief, his skeptical attitude as to whether such outlandish linguistic practice could exist, he might conclude, by cross-cultural comparative studies, that sexuality is held in low esteem in the English-speaking world.

One can forgive a society that borrowed from the language of excretion to describe filth and repulsion and things generally abhorrent. One can look with dismay, although not complete despair, on a society that appropriates the words that describe parts of the body and utilizes them as pejoratives. One can understand the use of language loaded with antagonistic double meanings to describe acts that are committed when men and women are erotically aroused.

It is possible to see the incalculable harm that such linguistic devices can accomplish—harm all the greater precisely because we are so often completely unaware not only of its source but also of its very existence—and yet understand, with a kindly forgivance, the social forces that have made such a linguistic development inevitable.

All this is not so tragic as to contemplate the use of the word *scum*. All that is repulsive and disgusting—to describe the life-giving fluid, the few drops of magical protoplasm in which are contained the fertilizer that, upon reaching the egg, alone can make another life.

Children, educated today in what many consider an atmosphere of enlightenment, when the mention of contraception, birth control, abortion, venereal disease, and homosexuality are encountered with increasing frequency, are expected by many to have free and uninhibited attitudes towards things sexual. Even the increased use of the once-forbidden words is itself considered an indicator, if not a cause, of this newer view of sex.

Yet, how can children not be repelled by their vision of sex, how can they not feel that they were begotten in sin, no matter how much the adult world may seek to educate them to the contrary, if the view of the world of reality is conditioned by a language which states that the semen is *scum*, and *scum* is all that is vile!

All that is vile and worthless—to describe the chemical substances necessary and sufficient for the generation of life, by which not only does mankind continue, but each man passes on, through his genes and chromosomes, his characteristics so that some of his individuality will continue in his child and in the human race.

And this is *scum!* That is what our language calls these most precious drops without which humanity could not continue. This is more than simple irony. It is bitter tragedy. This is more than a confession of man's contempt for sex, his view of sexuality as an abominable and generally dirty practice. It is a confession of his contempt for life—particularly and specifically his own, the human life.

And why not? Is this not the logic of his position? One starts with contempt for the body and its functions, and where can one end save with contempt for life contained in that body and sustained by those functions?

9

To the Victors Belong the Soiled

RANTED, as one might, that the dirty words associated with certain biological processes have been appropriated for nonbiological slang, and granted that these figurative meanings are almost invariably negative in quality, what is the explanation for this phenomenon? Is this proof that society reflects in its language a hostile attitude toward the biological acts, the organs that perform them, and the objects produced by them?

One might, perhaps, argue that the entire relationship is coincidental, for which there is little rebuttal, but it is a coincidence that defies the weight of the evidence. There are many indicators pointing unmistakably toward a causal relationship. In addition, there is a still greater abundance of evidence against the use of coincidence to explain phenomenological relationships that are found between language and culture.

Two other explanations might be made. The first is that slang may lend itself to be used for negative characterization, and elegant language for affirmation. This would, in fact, be in keeping with many studies of the origin of slang, in which the class differentiation is emphasized, with tabooed language arising from the least educated groups.

In English, however, such an explanation would run counter to the facts. There is slang for money (*dough*), for a sweetheart (*honey*), for energy (*ball of fire*), for success (*a feather in the cap*), and for almost all other desirable qualities.

Are there, however, sources of slang other than the terms also associated with the biological functions under discussion? Could the insults and the slurs have been found elsewhere? Indeed, they could, and sometimes they are. One borrows for negative connotations from the language of food, although there are positive connotations as well (*bread* and *bacon*, *applesauce* and *bologna*), from animal life (*to be a pig, to goose, to be a stoolpigeon*), from miscellaneous unclassifiable words and phrases (*to choke, to cut no ice*), and from coined words (*to be a slouch*).

There is no explanation for the appropriation of the biological dirty words for nonbiological negative qualities other than the simple and apparent one: the processes, the parts of the body, and the products are looked down upon, and therefore the improper language can properly be used only for other characteristics and persons held in low esteem.

The antibiological bias of modern culture, however, cannot be admitted; it is the more insidious because it is less openly faced. "What disturbs and alarms man are not the things," wrote Epictetus, "but his opinions and fancies about the things."

TWENTY-EIGHT

ONE HEARS a great deal about the necessity of calling a spade a spade—spoken by people who, of course, are not talking about spades. One hears about the need to teach children the facts of life—but how can Western man teach his children, or himself, the facts of life, when he is a prisoner of language, in which the very phrase *the facts of life* is a euphemism created to avoid saying *the facts of sex*!

Ours is a topsy-turvy language, saying what it does not

intend to say, or even the opposite of what it intends to say and yet with due deliberation. There are double meanings but each phrase in its context is clear and there is no ambiguity. The double meanings therefore fool no one, except that we are all conditioned by them, and so they fool everyone.

"It is impossible to estimate the social damage which has been done by the outworn taboos of obscenity," wrote Havelock Ellis.[1] "It is these taboos which have delayed until today the effort to combat venereal diseases and the discussion of the population question. The names of the evils were too 'obscene' to mention and therefore the evils themselves were allowed to flourish unchecked."

Walt Whitman said that the obscene words should be collected and placed in dictionaries,[2] and years later Robert Graves protested that, in a work devoted to the social good of swearing, he could not even mention the words under discussion: "I have yielded to the society in which I move which is an obscene society: that is it acquiesces emotionally in the validity of the taboo, while intellectually objecting to it."[3]

The unmentionables have long been mentioned, the unwhisperables have long been whispered, but the unprintables have only recently been printed. Graves could not print them, but many years earlier Smollett could write of "two certain words":

> They cannot, my dear mother, said the novice, be pronounced at all; they will make all the blood in one's body fly up into one's face.—But you may whisper them in my ear, quoth the abbess.[4]

A serious scientific work on linguistics, with several chapters devoted to tabooed language and specifically to modern taboos, not only fails to mention the obscene words, but omits any hint that they exist as a group. So tabooed are the words, for these writers, that even the subject of tabooed words is itself taboo![5]

Legman and many others have protested that it is impossible to report folklore with any degree of fidelity so long as the taboos exist. "No interested person can have failed to notice that nothing authentically folk can withstand the acid rot of prettification and faking in its translation from fact into print." [6] To which the editor of the scholarly journal in which this appeared makes a footnote: "The Canadian Criminal Code has made it necessary to delete thirty-six lines of verse from the examples given in this article. These lines, of course, deal with the very thing about which the author writes."

We have long been honoring the taboos in the violation, not in the practice. There have even been laws against swearing, punishable by fines and imprisonment, and for those who wish to follow the absurd story of these restrictions, Johnson has summarized them.[7]

What is obscene? The question is answered succinctly by Weston La Barre: "Nothing is obscene that has not been previously defined culturally as such." [8]

But the definition is not something that exists in a dictionary; it is the internalization of the concept of obscenity into the minds of the people, and nothing is so powerful to force this upon us as language.

Once no work of literature could appear, no matter how serious the author or how lofty his motive, if it contained any of the tabooed terminology. Today, there is the new Merriam Webster Dictionary,[9] with *cunt* and *shit* and *prick,* among others, spelled out without asterisks or dashes, and Mario Pei uses the pages of the *New York Times* to protest that *fuck* is omitted, although he carefully writes his review in such a way that the omitted word is never mentioned.[10]

No longer are there any unprintables, except for those who do not care to print them. We have come to believe that perhaps the banishment was worse than the thing banished. As Robert W. Haney put it:

> Our blushes and smirks and self-righteous denunciations of four-letter words, lewd pictures, and all the other paraphernalia of obscenity and pornography are little more than the attempt to feel noble when we are really being absurd. And we pass on through generations this legacy of fear. All the muck and dirt which pornographic literature and photography can pour into our bookstores or onto our newsstands is trivial beside the real damage to the human soul—the systematic production of frightened and inept men and women which goes under the name of censorship.[11]

Until the epoch-making decision of Judge Woolsey which permitted legal publication and distribution of James Joyce's *Ulysses* in America, the prohibited terminology had never appeared except in under-the-counter publications. However, it was not until *The Naked and the Dead* and *From Here to Eternity* that authors used the words abundantly.

From Here to Eternity would be worthy of separate study in the development of pornographic language, for within its pages almost every figurative nonbiological use is made of the tabooed words, or at least of those that were able to pass the censor.[12] In itself, this novel is almost a dictionary (or at least a compendium) of once-prohibited terminology.

This does not mean, however, that its author did not suffer the fate of expurgation. *Fuck* and *shit* had to be reduced in number considerably (by about fifty per cent) before the publisher permitted their use, while *prick* and *cunt* (printable by Merriam Webster which excludes *fuck*) were not allowed to see the light of day. Nevertheless, the cleansing process did not prevent *Life* magazine from declaring:

> And here, of course, we get to the four-letter words. *From Here to Eternity* has more of them per page than any other novel ever published for general reading in this country. The excuse is that the soldier talks that way, so any true account of the soldier's talk, life and habitat must include the characteristic monosyllables in more or less accurate proportion.[13]

However, *Life* goes on to say, Stephen Crane, Kipling and Tolstoy managed to convey the feelings, the truth, and even the sound of the soldiers without resorting to "lingual paresis," and then adds:

> This particular brand of "realism" is phony, anyhow. Four-letter words in print, especially when they occur with the clamorous repetition of *From Here to Eternity*,

take on an emphasis and a total significance which they do not have in the actual life and language of the soldier. There, as anyone who has been in or around armies knows, they are blurred and minimized by the frequency of their use. Printing magnifies them, and the result is a misleading falseness which is the opposite of valid realism! [13]

Alas, Jones was thwarted in his efforts to achieve realism through frequency of usage, and thus to blur the edges of his sharp pen and of the sharp-tongued soldiers. For in the 859 pages, *fuck* was reduced from 258 mentions to 108, *shit* was reduced from 135 to a mere 50, and *cunt* and *prick,* which appeared many times in the original manuscript, were eliminated by the cleansers.[14]

Just a short time before the appearance of *From Here to Eternity,* Bernard De Voto,[15] in Harper's Magazine, took note of the relaxation of word taboos. Talking of Mark Twain's use of some prohibited words in his charming ribaldry, *1601,*[16] De Voto noted that "the taboo of those monosyllables remained almost though not quite absolute till about 1930, when it began to relax." Toleration of the monosyllables, occasional and even habitual use of them, he noted, "has come to signify frankness, sophistication, liberalness, companionability, and even smartness among a very great many educated and well-to-do metropolitan women."

This development, by which the words are used with ever-increasing frequency and abandon, has not continued without protest. Robert E. Fitch,[17] Dean of Religion at the Pacific School of Religion, lashes out in fury against dealing with certain matters on the "one-syllable four-letter level," instead of utilization of three syllables which permit the same matters to be "viewed with abstract and antiseptic propriety." It is the pose of sophistication and urbanity, writes Dean Fitch, under a headline in which the French equivalent of *shit* (i.e., *merde*) may have been used in the largest type face in history, except for the scrawls on toilet walls.

We have reached the stage where nothing is taboo, everything goes, or at least so it seems. The employment of obscenity, says Albert Ellis, who puts *obscenity* in quotes, "is that mode of sex behavior which probably has the distinction of being, at one and the same time, the most widely condemned and condoned American sex practice." [18]

Once-tabooed words are now spoken with abandon, and are found in novels, sometimes pronounced on stage, and no dictionary is complete without them. It is a long road that led to *From Here to Eternity*; after all, it is less than 250 years since Alexander Pope's well-known couplet:

> *Immodest words admit of no defence,*
> *For want of Decency is want of sense.*

Today the words no longer shock. The taboo is omnipresent, but recognized more in its violation than in its acceptance. But it is time to stop and ask ourselves: what does it all mean?

TWENTY-NINE

EVERYWHERE we are surrounded by the tabooed words, yet they are not the less tabooed. Modern man is frightened by them, as if they were evil symbols, just as primitive man was frightened by superstitions and magical symbols.

Philip Wylie[19] has depicted the panic that would ensue if people were suddenly confronted with these words and were compelled to acknowledge their existence openly. "Contrary to expectation, the end of civilization came about through a series of events connected in no way with war or atomic bombardment," but with cloud formations and stars that threw first Chicago, and then the rest of the world into panic, by forming a series of forbidden words: *nuts, crap, shit, merde.* Some proposed that atomic bombs be used to disperse the naughty clouds, others stated that the words "represent the imminence of the Day of Judgment and the approach of the Opening of the Gates of Paradise." Finally, a new star appears, and then another, and it is seen that the stars have formed "an unimaginably vast initial of their own," an F of truly astronomical magnitude.

THIRTY

HE PURITANS, the Comstocks, the self-appointed and self-anointed guardians of the morals, proclaim that the world is being corrupted by the widespread pornography. What started with the legal publication of Joyce, Lawrence, and Miller ends with the hard-core pornography, the crude comic books, the under-the-counter business with which our youth is being smuttered. And the crusaders for a new era in sexual freedom, for a relaxed attitude toward sexual behavior and pleasure, for the most part see evidence of progress in the wider use of the obscene symbols.

Alas, the puritans who are so willing to concede defeat have actually won their greatest victories, and the liberals and libertarians are defeating their own ends each time they exult in victory.

For the language about which so much debate rages is actually antisexual and puritanical. The more obscene it is, the more it reinforces the puritanical codes that are reflected in the idiom and internalized in the minds of users, writers, speakers, and readers.

The words can find their way into dictionaries, but if the words for the biological processes are made synonymous with all things dirty and abhorrent, people will see the processes and organs as dirty and abhorrent, and the more the words are used, the more will they structure their reality in this way. Our antibiological biases are being strengthened by the downfall of censorship, because language reflects and reinforces these biases even while the phrases are being banned.

Only a campaign to change the language, as Albert Ellis[20] and a few others have been leading, will save modern man from the fate that—win, draw, or lose in the struggle against censorship—the liberals must lose in the struggle against puritanism.

Unless one changes the very structure of the language in which obscenities are used, the wider are these words spread among the people, the more will their rigid attitudes toward the body and its functions be reinforced.

The puritans are losing every battle, but they can be cocksure of winning the war.

Meanings, wrote Sapir, are "not so much discovered in experience as imposed upon it, because of the tyrannical hold that linguistic form has upon our orientation in the world." [21]

The linguistic system, wrote Whorf,[22] is the shaper of ideas, not merely the mirror of them.

That is why, if a change is to come about in the image that man holds of the human body and its functions, there must be a conscious effort to alter the language of obscenities.

We are slaves of language, not its masters, and perhaps the first stage in any struggle for freedom must be a recognition that the state of slavery exists.

Footnotes, Elaborations, and Explanations

I. TABOOS WITHOUT TOTEMS

1. Edward Sapir: *Culture, Language and Personality*, U. of California Press, Berkeley and Los Angeles, 1960, p. 11. (Original publication, 1933.)

2. *Ibid.*, p. 76. (Original publication, 1929.)

3. *Ibid.*, p. 68-69. (Original publication, 1929.)

4. Benjamin Lee Whorf: *Language, Thought, and Reality*, Technology Press of M.I.T. and John Wiley & Sons, New York, 1959, p. 213-4. (Original publication, 1940.) The emphasis is in the original.

5. Robert Briffault: *The Mothers: A Study of the Origins of Sentiments and Institutions*, 3 vols., Macmillan, New York, 1927, vol. 2, p. 31.

6. *Ibid.*

7. Edward Sapir, *op. cit.*, p. 68. (Original publication, 1929.)

8. A. R. Radcliffe-Brown, "Introduction to the Analysis of Kinship Systems," in Norman W. Bell and Ezra F. Vogel: *A Modern Introduction to the Family,* Free Press, Glencoe, Ill., 1960, p. 224. (Original publication, 1950.)

9. Duncan R. MacKenzie: *The Spirit-Ridden Konde,* Seeley, Service & Co., London, 1925, p. 297.

10. Information obtained through the library of the Institute for Sex Research, Bloomington, Ind., based on the work of Phillip Ludwig Hanneken, in Albert H. Sallengre: *Novus Thesaurus Antiquitatum Romanarum,* 3 vols., 1716-1719.

11. Henri Alexandre Junod: *The Life of a South African Tribe,* 2nd ed., Macmillan, London, 1927. (Original publication in French, 1898.)

12. Knud Leem, "An Account of the Laplanders of Finmark," in J. Pinkerton: *A General Collection of the Best and Most Interesting Voyages and Travels in All Parts of the World,* Longman, Hurst, London, 17 vols., 1808-1814, vol. 1, p. 486.

13. A. A. Macdonell, "Vedic Religion," in James Hastings, ed.: *Encyclopaedia of Religion and Ethics,* Scribner's, New York, 1922, vol. 12, p. 616.

14. Allen Walker Read: *Lexical Evidence from Folk Epigraphy in Western North America: A Glossarial Study of the Low Element in the English Vocabulary,* privately published, Paris 1935, p. 11; from Walter Roth: *Ethnological Studies among the North-West-Central Queensland Aborigines,* p. 184.

15. E. E. Evans-Pritchard, "Some Collective Expressions of Obscenity in Africa," *Journal, Royal Anthropological Institute of Great Britain and Ireland,* 1929, 59, 311-31.

16. James Frazer: *The Golden Bough,* 1890; the references are to *The New Golden Bough,* Criterion Books, New York, 1959, p. 190.

17. *Idem.*

18. *Idem.*

19. *Ibid.,* p. 193.

20. Leonard Bloomfield: *Language,* Holt, New York, 1933, p. 155.

21. Exodus, xx, 4.

22. Exodus, xx, 7.

23. G. K. Chesterton, "On the Prudery of Slang," in *All Is Grist; A Book of Essays,* Methuen & Co., London, 1931, p. 1-5.

24. The relationship between social classes and slang has been the subject of many studies. An early work was that of Hotten, 1865 (*see bibliography*). A rather lengthy study of the subject is found in Eric Partridge: *Slang To-day and Yesterday,* Macmillan, New York, 1934.

25. For a brief examination of the subject from the Marxist point-of-view, see the pages on slang in Margaret Schlauch: *The Gift of Tongues,* Modern Age Books, New York, 1942.

26. Bloomfield, *op. cit.*

27. Maurice Weseen: *Dictionary of American Slang,* Thomas Y. Crowell, New York, 1934.

28. Hyman E. Goldin, ed.: *Dictionary of American Underworld Lingo,* Twayne, New York, 1950.

29. There is a considerable literature on the ethnic epithet, including an entire book devoted to this subject: A. A. Roback: *A Dictionary of International Slurs (Ethnophaulisms),* Sci-Art Publishers, Cambridge, Mass., 1944. The bibliographical references are covered thoroughly in W. J. Burke: *The Literature of Slang,* New York Public Library, New York, 1939. The subject is discussed by H. L. Mencken, oddly enough under the heading of "Euphemisms," in *The American Language,* 4th ed., Knopf, New York, 1936 (original publication, 1919) and in his *Supplement I, The American Language,* same publisher, 1945. Mencken's footnotes will supply the reader with literature references, up to 1945, on the specifically American aspects of the ethnic epithet.

30. Among those who have investigated the corruption of religious words into English-language slang are Elijah Clarence Hills, "Exclamations in American English," *Dialect Notes,* 1924, 5, 253-84, and Mencken, *op. cit.,* under the heading "Expletives."

31. See Burke, *op. cit.,* for early bibliography on this subject. The reference to *Oh, my* comes from Burges Johnson: *The Lost Art of Profanity,* Bobbs-Merrill Co., Indianapolis and New York, 1948, p. 26.

32. This usage of the forbidden words in both biological and non-biological connotations is pointed out by A. W. Read, *op. cit.,* and by Albert Ellis, in Paul Krassner's *Impolite Interviews,* Lyle Stuart, New York, 1961. It is briefly mentioned by Henry and Freda Thornton: *How to Achieve Sex Happiness in Marriage,* Vanguard Press, New

York, 1939: "Whenever the organs and functions of sex, as well as those of excretion, have been covered with a mantle of shame, the words used to designate them have also, of course, been considered shameful," and the writers point out that many of these expressions are "objectionable (to a sociologist) because their indirection or their double meaning imply and perpetuate an attitude of shame." The use of forbidden sexual terms for expressions of deceit and cheating is examined by Wentworth and Flexner (*see bibliography*). There seems to have been little or no attention paid to this phenomenon, so far as this writer can determine, except for brief mention in the above-cited passages.

33. Walt Whitman: *An American Primer*, Small, Maynard & Co., Boston, 1904.

34. Edward Sapir, *op. cit.*, pp. 68-69. (Original publication, 1929.)

II. THE HANDWRITING ON THE WALL

1. Allen Walker Read, *op. cit.*, p. 5.

2. For a popular presentation of the changing attitude toward sexual terminology, both accepted and forbidden, see William Iversen, "A Short History of Swearing," *Playboy*, vol. 8, Sept. 1961, p. 101. It may be of interest to note that Iversen's article could not have been published were it not for the sophistication whose force and power he questions.

3. Otto Jespersen, "Veiled Language," *Society for Pure English*, Tract #33, Oxford, 1929, pp. 420-30.

4. Through Iversen, *op. cit.*, I learn that Norman Mailer has given the phonetic spelling *fug* to the most used four-letter word of all, reducing to a mere three letters the only true four-letter word in existence.

5. The history of how one four-letter word traveled from tongue to tongue is traced by Allen Walker Read in "An Obscenity Symbol," *American Speech*, 1934, 9, 264-78.

6. *Webster's Third New International Dictionary of the English Language*, Merriam Co., Springfield, Mass., 1961, suggests that *piss* came from the Vulgar Latin through the Old French to the Middle English, and traces *shit* from Old English and Middle English.

7. Richard Paget: *Human Speech,* Harcourt, Brace, New York, 1930.

8. Lester V. Berrey and Melvin Van den Bark: *The American Thesaurus of Slang,* Thomas Y. Crowell, New York, 1945.

9. *Webster's Third New International Dictionary, op. cit.,* p. 1665.

10. Eric Partridge, editor: *A Classical Dictionary of the Vulgar Tongue,* by Captain Grose, issued for private subscribers by the Scholartis Press, 1931.

11. It is interesting to note that all of these initials appear in a recent book of abbreviations, but that only the respectable antecedents are given, with no hint of any other words or phrases to which the abbreviations might fit. *Life,* in a very brief review of the book in its issue of Aug. 1, 1961, singles out *t.s., p.o.'ed, snafu,* as worthy of special note.

12. Berrey and Van den Bark, *op. cit.*

13. Mitford M. Mathews, ed.: *A Dictionary of Americanisms on Historical Principles,* 2 vols., University of Chicago Press, Chicago, 1951, vol. 2, p. 1523; *see also* W. L. McAtee: *Nomina Abitera,* privately printed, 1945, pp. 25-30, for discussion of *shitepoke.*

14. Captain Grose: *A Dictionary of Buckish Slang, University Wit, and Pickpocket Eloquence,* printed for C. Chappell, London, 1811; *see also* footnote 10, this chapter, *supra.*

15. Harold Wentworth and Stuart Berg Flexner: *Dictionary of American Slang,* Thomas Y. Crowell, New York, 1960.

16. John S. Farmer: *Slang and Its Analogues, Past and Present,* 7 vols., London, 1890. The later volumes have the name of W. E. Henley as collaborator.

17. Berrey and Van den Bark, *op. cit.*

18. A. Barrère: *Argot and Slang: A New French and English Dictionary,* Chiswick Press by C. Wittingham and Co., London, 1887.

19. J. H. Huizinga: *Confessions of a European in England,* Heinemann, London, 1958, p. 44-45.

20. An objection has been raised by one of my readers that it is difficult to accept the explanations here offered and at the same time account for the somewhat synonymous expression: *he turned green.* The latter is, of course, idiomatic and figurative, but hardly forbidden. Greenness, in this instance, represents pallor: the fright is so great that

he lost all the color in his face; one can compare this to the similar expression: *he turned white*. There is, of course, no contradiction between equating fright with involuntarily losing the color in one's face by a flow of blood, and involuntarily defecating, by loss of muscular control. In both instances, the language is saying that the fright was so great that it overcame the normal physiological processes of the body. Furthermore, slang is not in itself a closed and self-consistent system. Its only consistency, in fact, that we have found is the one that is the subject of this study.

21. *New York Times,* Sept. 9, 1961, p. 22.

22. Robert Graves: *Lars Porsena or the Future of Swearing and Improper Language,* Dutton, New York, 1927, p. 17, 50. The revised edition of this essay was entitled: *The Future of Swearing and Improper Language,* K. Paul, Trench Trubner, London, 1936.

23. H. L. Mencken, *op. cit.,* 1936, p. 304.

24. H. L. Mencken, *op. cit.,* 1945, p. 640.

25. Mario Pei: *The Story of Language,* J. B. Lippincott, Philadelphia and New York, 1949, p. 251.

26. Vance Randolph and George P. Wilson: *Down in the Holler: A Gallery of Ozark. Folk Speech,* University of Oklahoma Press, Norman, Okla., 1953, p. 101.

27. Berrey and Van den Bark, *op. cit.*

28. I am indebted to my nephew, Alan B. Sagarin, an ex-Marine, for this information.

29. From Randolph and Wilson, *op. cit.,* p. 117.

III. THE POLICY OF THE BIG STICK

1. Duncan MacDougald, Jr., "Language and Sex," in Albert Ellis and Albert Abarbanel, editors: *The Encyclopedia of Sexual Behavior,* 2 vols., Hawthorn Books, New York, 1961, vol. 2, p. 586-7.

2. Paget, *op. cit.,* Chapter 8, "Vowel and Consonant Symbolism."

3. Alfred R. Wallace, "The Expressiveness of Speech, or Mouth-Gesture as a Factor in the Origin of Language," *Fortnightly Review,* 1895, 64, (n.s. 58), 528-43.

4. *New York Times,* Oct. 2, 1935.

5. Mencken, *The American Language, op. cit.,* p. 307.

6. Graves, *op. cit.,* p. 19.

7. Mencken, *op. cit.,* pp. 300-1.

8. For the information dealing with Spanish-language obscenities, I am indebted to Mr. Gonzales Segura.

9. Vance Randolph: *Vulgar Rhymes from the Ozarks,* 1954, unpublished manuscript. The typescript of this work was examined in the library of the Institute for Sex Research, Bloomington, Indiana.

10. Justinian (pseud.): *Americana Sexualis,* privately printed, Chicago (1939).

11. (Anon.) *A New Canting Dictionary Comprehending All the Terms Ancient and Modern, Used in the Several Tribes of Gypsies, Beggars,* etc., privately printed, London, 1725.

12. Leonard Bloomfield, *op. cit.,* p. 396.

13. Randolph and Wilson, *op. cit.,* p. 113

14. *Idem.*

15. Mencken, *op. cit.,* 1936, p. 301.

IV. STICKS AND STONES WILL BREAK MY BONES

1. For an early study of this subject, see Marie Gladys Hayden, "Terms of Disparagement in American Dialect Speech," *Dialect Notes,* 1915, 4, 194-223; *see also footnote* 29, chapter one.

2. A mere counting of the number of synonyms for terms of disparagement in the modern slang dictionaries will convince the reader of the richness of the English language in this area.

3. *See* Wentworth and Flexner, *op. cit.,* for excellent material on this word.

4. H. N. Cary: *Sexual Vocabulary,* 5 vols., unpublished, not dated, *ca.* 1916. The typescript was examined in the Institute for Sex Research, Bloomington, Indiana. Another work by Cary, likewise unpublished, is to be found at Bloomington: *Introduction to Sexual Vocabulary,* 2 vols., Chicago, 1920.

5. Berrey and Van den Bark, *op. cit.*

6. *Idem.*

7. Donald Webster Cory: *The Homosexual in America: A Subjective Approach,* Greenberg, New York, 1951, p. 105; 2nd ed., Castle Books,

8. Robert A. Harper, "Psychological Aspects of Homosexuality," address delivered before the Society for the Scientific Study of Sex, New York, May 22, 1959.

9. Cory, *op. cit.*

V. EUPHEMIST, WHAT'S THE GOOD WORD?

1. Burke, *op. cit.*

2. Read, *op. cit.,* p. 14.

3. A. Carnoy: *La Science du Mot: Traité de Sémantique,* Editions "Universitas," Louvain, 1927, p. 351.

4. D. H. Lawrence: *Pornography and Obscenity,* Knopf, New York, 1930, p. 22.

5. Natalie F. Joffe, "The Vernacular of Menstruation," *Word,* Dec. 1948, 4, 181-6.

6. Bronislaw Malinowski: *Sex and Repression in Savage Society,* Meridian Books, New York, 1955, p. 62. (Original publication, 1927.) 1960.

VI. LUV IS A THREE-LETTER WORD

1. Albert Ellis: *The American Sexual Tragedy,* Lyle Stuart, New York, 1962. (Original publication, 1954.)

2. David Riesman, with Nathan Glazer and Reuel Denney: *The Lonely Crowd,* abridged by the authors, Doubleday, New York, 1953, p. 96*ff.* (Original publication, 1950.)

3. Randolph and Wilson, *op. cit.,* p. 113.

4. Berrey and Van den Bark, *op. cit.*

5. Mathews, *op. cit.*

6. Wentworth and Flexner, *op. cit.*

7. Carl Jefferson Weber: *English-American Dictionary*, 1917, unpublished manuscript, p. 85; this information was brought to my attention by Allen Walker Read, who likewise pointed out to me the citation from Elliot, below.

8. Andrew G. Elliot: *Hell! I'm British: Plain Man Looks at America, Americans and Englishmen*, Musson Book Co., Toronto, 1939, p. 83.

9. Riesman *et al., op. cit.,* p. 170.

10. *New York Times,* Nov. 25, 1961, p. 21.

11. Partridge, 1931, *op. cit.*

12. Cary, *op. cit.*

13. Eric Partridge: *Shakespeare's Bawdy: A Literary and Psychological Essay and a Comprehensive Glossary*, Routledge, London, 1947, p. 118; and Carl Darling Buck: *A Dictionary of Selected Synonyms in the Principal Indo-European Languages: A Contribution to the History of Ideas,* University of Chicago Press, Chicago, 1949.

14. Farmer, *op. cit.*

15. H. L. Mencken, *op. cit.,* 1936, p. 312.

16. Farmer, *op. cit.*

17. Albert Ellis, "An Impolite Interview," *The Realist,* May 1960; reprinted in Paul Krassner: *Impolite Interviews,* Lyle Stuart, New York, 1961, pp. 30-31.

VII. LINGUISTICS: EROTICA AND CURIOSA

1. Ashley Montagu: *Man: His First Million Years,* World Publishing Co., Cleveland and New York, 1957, p. 117.

2. Mencken, *op. cit.,* p. 315-6.

3. Alan Sillitoe: *Saturday Night and Sunday Morning,* Knopf, New York, 1959, p. 124.

4. John Wain: *Living in the Present,* Secker & Warburg, London, 1955, p. 19.

5. Julian Franklyn: *The Cockney: A Survey of London Life and Language,* A. Deutsch, London, 1953.

6. Sam Boal, *New York Post,* June 21, 1947, p. 5.

7. Harold Wentworth: " 'Sandwich' Words and Rime-Caused Nonce Words," *Philological Studies, West Virginia University Bulletin,* Sept. 1939, 40, 65-71.

8. Edward Sapir: *Language: An Introduction to the Study of Speech,* Harcourt, Brace, New York, 1949, p. 72. (Original publication, 1921.)

9. I am indebted to my friend, John Phillips Horton, for this information.

10. Weseen, *op. cit.,* p. 301.

11. Frederick Packard, "Schizoverbia," *New Yorker,* Jan. 12, 1946, 83-84.

12. H. W. Fowler: *A Dictionary of Modern English Usage,* Clarendon Press, Oxford, 1937, p. 624; *see also* Margaret Nicholson: *A Dictionary of American-English Usage Based on Fowler's Modern English Usage,* Oxford, New York, 1957, p. 593.

13. Mario Pei and Frank Gaynor: *A Dictionary of Linguistics,* Philosophical Library, New York, 1954, p. 218.

VIII. IN THE BEGINNING THERE WAS A SEED

1. Wentworth and Flexner, *op. cit.,* p. 132.

2. I am informed that this usage is rather limited in the United States to the East coast, to urbanized areas, and to immigrants and first- and second-generation Americans. Several readers, hailing from the South, Mid-West, and Far West, inform me that they had (*a*) never heard the word used in this manner before reaching New York, or (*b*) never heard the word used in this manner before reading this manuscript. I am pleasantly surprised to learn of the confinement of this practice to a limited segment of the American population.

IX. TO THE VICTORS BELONG THE SOILED

1. Havelock Ellis: *The Revaluation of Obscenity,* Hours Press, Paris, 1931, p. 25. This essay has been reprinted at various times; *see* bibliography for American publication.

2. Whitman, *op. cit.*

3. R. Graves, *op. cit.*, p. 53.

4. From Burges Johnson, *op. cit.*

5. Robert M. Estrich and Hans Sperber: *Three Keys to Language,* Rinehart, New York, 1952.

6. G. Legman, "The Bawdy Song . . . in Fact and in Print," *Explorations* (published by the University of Toronto, Canada), 7, pp. 139-56.

7. Johnson, *op. cit.*, p. 41*ff.*

8. Weston La Barre, "Obscenity: An Anthropological Appraisal," *Law and Contemporary Problems,* 20, Autumn 1955, pp. 533-43.

9. *Webster's Third New International Dictionary, op. cit.*

10. Mario Pei, review of *Webster's Third New International Dictionary of the English Language, New York Times Book Review,* Oct. 22, 1961, p. 6.

11. Robert W. Haney: *Comstockery in America: Patterns of Censorship and Control,* Beacon Press, Boston, 1960, p. 65.

12. James Jones: *From Here to Eternity,* Scribner's, New York, 1951.

13. *Life,* April 16, 1951, p. 40.

14. The information contained in this paragraph comes from an unimpeachable but private source.

15. Bernard De Voto, "The Easy Chair," *Harper's,* Dec. 1948, 197, 98-101.

16. Mark Twain: *Conversation as it Was by the Social Fireside in the Time of the Tudors (1601),* privately printed for Lyle Stuart, New York (1962). (Original publication, 1880).

17. Robert E. Fitch, "La Mystique de la Merde," *New Republic,* Sept. 3, 1956, 135, 17-18.

18. Albert Ellis: *The Folklore of Sex,* Grove Press, New York, 1961, p. 134. (Original publication, 1951.)

19. Philip Wylie: *Opus 21,* Rinehart, New York, 1949, p. 199-219. I should like to acknowledge my debt to Barry Sheer for calling this delightful section of Wylie's book to my attention.

20. Albert Ellis, "An Impolite Interview," *op. cit.*

21. Edward Sapir, "Conceptual Categories in Primitive Languages," *Science*, 1931, 74, 578; quoted by Harry Hoijer, "The Sapir-Whorf Hypothesis," in Harry Hoijer, ed.: *Language in Culture*, University of Chicago Press, Chicago, 1954, p. 94.

22. Benjamin Lee Whorf, "The Relation of Habitual Thought and Behavior to Language," in Leslie Spier, ed.: *Language, Culture and Personality: Essays in Memory of Edward Sapir*, Sapir Memorial Publication Fund, Menasha, Wisc., 1941, p. 75-93; reprinted in B. L. Whorf: *Language, Thought, and Reality, op. cit.*, pp. 134-59. (Originally written, 1939.)

BIBLIOGRAPHY AND REFERENCES

The following books and articles have been included in this bibliography:

1. All books and articles mentioned in the footnotes and referring to the text, except for some minor newspaper and magazine references.

2. Books and articles on obscenity that the author has found useful, and would recommend for further study of the subject, but which have not been referred to in the text and footnotes.

3. Books and articles of value, dealing with linguistics in general, and with the relationship of language to culture specifically,

which are recommended for further study, but which have not been referred to in the text and footnotes.

Abarbanel, Albert, *see* Ellis, Albert, and Abarbanel, Albert.

Barrère, A., *Argot and Slang: A New French and English Dictionary*, Chiswick Press by C. Wittingham and Co., London, 1887.

Bell, Norman W., and Vogel, Ezra F., *A Modern Introduction to the Family*, Free Press, Glencoe, Ill., 1960.

Bennet, Kathryn S., "Slang, Latin vs. American," *Classical Journal*, 31, October 1935, pp. 35-41.

Berrey, Lester V., and Van den Bark, Melvin, *The American Thesaurus of Slang*, Thomas Y. Crowell, New York, 1945.

Blanshard, Paul, *The Right to Read: The Battle Against Censorship*, Beacon Press, Boston, 1955.

Bloomfield, Leonard, *Language*, Holt, New York, 1933; originally published under the title *An Introduction to the Study of Language*, Holt, New York, 1914.

Bloomfield, Leonard, "Linguistic Aspects of Science," *International Encyclopedia of Unified Science*, 1(4), 1939.

Bodmer, Frederick, *The Loom of Language*, Norton, New York, 1944.

Bok, Curtis, "Censorship and the Arts," in Wilcox, Claire, ed., *Civil Liberties under Attack, q.v.*

Bram, Joseph, *Language and Society*, Doubleday, Garden City, 1955.

Briffault, Robert, *The Mothers: A Study of the Origins of Sentiments and Institutions*, 3 vols., Macmillan, New York, 1927.

Bryan, George S., "Cant in Language," *Quarterly Journal of Speech Education*, 6, June 1920, pp. 79-82.

Buck, Carl Darling, *A Dictionary of Selected Synonyms in the Principal Indo-European Languages: A Contribution to the History of Ideas,* U. of Chicago Press, Chicago, 1949.

Burke, W. J., *The Literature of Slang,* New York Public Library, New York, 1939.

Carnoy, A., *La Science du mot: Traité de sémantique,* Edition "Universitas," Louvain, 1927.

Cary, H. N., *Introduction to Sexual Vocabulary,* 2 vols., unpublished, Chicago, 1920; typescript at Institute for Sex Research, Inc., Bloomington, Ind.

Cary, H. N., *Sexual Vocabulary,* 5 vols., unpublished, not dated (*ca.* 1916); typescript at Institute for Sex Research, Inc., Bloomington, Ind.

Cassirer, Ernst, *An Essay on Man,* Yale U. Press, New Haven, 1944.

Cassirer, Ernst, *Language and Myth,* Harper, New York, 1946.

Chase, Stuart, and Chase, Marian T., *Power of Words,* Harcourt, Brace, New York, 1954.

Chase, Stuart, *The Tyranny of Words,* Harcourt, Brace, New York, 1938.

Chesterton, G. K., *All is Grist: A Book of Essays,* Methuen, London, 1931.

Clemens, S. L., *see* Twain, Mark.

Conant, R. W., "Classic Slang," *The Dial,* 20, Feb. 1, 1896, p. 63.

Cory, Donald Webster, *The Homosexual in America: A Subjective Approach,* Greenberg, New York, 1951; 2nd ed., Castle Books, New York, 1960.

Crawley, Alfred Ernest, *Studies of Savages and Sex*, Methuen, London, 1929.

Denney, Reuel, *see* Reisman, David, with Glazer, Nathan, and Denney, Reuel.

De Voto, Bernard, "The Easy Chair," *Harper's*, 197, December 1948, pp. 98-101.

Diamond, A. S., *The History and Origin of Language*, Philosophical Society, New York, 1959.

Elliot, Andrew G., *Hell! I'm British: Plain Man Looks at America, Americans and Englishmen*, Musson Book Co., Toronto, 1939.

Ellis, Albert, "An Impolite Interview," *The Realist*, May 1960; reprinted in Krassner, Paul, *Impolite Interviews, q.v.*

Ellis, Albert, *The American Sexual Tragedy*, Lyle Stuart, New York, 1962.

Ellis, Albert, *The Folklore of Sex*, Grove Press, New York, 1961.

Ellis, Albert, and Abarbanel, Albert, eds., *The Encyclopedia of Sexual Behavior*, 2 vols., Hawthorn Books, New York, 1961.

Ellis, Havelock, *The Revaluation of Obscenity*, Hours Press, Paris, 1931; reprinted in *More Essays of Love and Virtue*, Doubleday, Doran, New York, 1931, and *On Life and Sex: Essays of Love and Virtue*, Garden City Publishing Co., Garden City, 1937.

Entwistle, William J., *Aspects of Language*, Faber and Faber, London, 1953.

Ernst, Morris L., and Seagle, William, *To the Pure . . . A Study of Obscenity and the Censor*, Viking Press, New York, 1928.

Estrich, Robert M., and Sperber, Hans, *Three Keys to Language,* Rinehart, New York, 1952.

Evans-Pritchard, E. E., "Some Collective Expressions of Obscenity in Africa," *Journal, Royal Anthropological Institute of Great Britain and Ireland,* 59, 1929, pp. 311-331.

Farmer, John S., with Henley, W. E., *Slang and Its Analogues, Past and Present,* 7 vols., London, 1890-1894.

Fitch, Robert E., "La Mystique de la Merde," *New Republic,* 135, September, 3, 1956, pp. 17-18; *see also* comment in *Time,* October 1, 1956.

Flexner, Stuart Berg, *see* Wentworth, Harold, and Flexner, Stuart Berg.

Fowler, H. W., *A Dictionary of Modern English Usage,* Clarendon Press, Oxford, 1937.

Franklyn, Julian, *The Cockney: A Survey of London Life and Language,* A. Deutsch, London, 1953.

Frazer, James, *The Golden Bough,* 1890; abridged edition, *The New Golden Bough,* Criterion Books, New York, 1959.

Gaynor, Frank, *see* Pei, Mario, and Gaynor, Frank.

Glazer, Nathan, *see* Riesman, David, with Glazer, Nathan, and Denney, Reuel.

Goldin, Hyman E., ed., *Dictionary of American Slang,* Thomas Y. Crowell, New York, 1934.

Graves, Robert, *Lars Porsena or the Future of Swearing and Improper Language,* Dutton, New York, 1927; revised edition, *The Future of Swearing and Improper Language,* K. Paul, Trench, Trubner, London, 1936.

Grose, Captain, *A Dictionary of Buckish Slang, University Wit, and Pickpocket Eloquence,* C. Chappell, London, 1811; *see also* Partridge, Eric, ed., *A Classical Dictionary, infra.*

Hallowell, A. Irving, *see* Spier, Leslie, Hallowell, A. Irving, and Newman, Stanley S.

Haney, Robert W., *Comstockery in America: Patterns of Censorship and Control,* Beacon Press, Boston, 1960.

Hanneken, Phillip Ludwig, *in* Sallengre, Albert H., *Novus Thesaurus Antiquitatum Romanarum, q. v.*

Harper, Robert A., "Psychological Aspects of Homosexuality," address delivered before Society for the Scientific Study of Sex, New York, May 22, 1959.

Hastings, James, ed., *Encyclopaedia of Religion and Ethics,* Scribner's, New York, 1922.

Hayakawa, S. I., *Language in Thought and Action,* Harcourt, Brace, New York, 1949; original title, *Language in Action,* 1939.

Hayden, Marie Gladys, "Terms of Disparagement in American Dialect Speech," *Dialect Notes,* 4, 1915, pp. 194-223.

Henley, W. E., *see* Farmer, John S., with Henley, W. E.

Hills, Elijah Clarence, "Exclamations in American English," *Dialect Notes,* 5, 1924, pp. 253-284.

Hoijer, Harry, ed., *Language in Culture,* U. of Chicago Press, Chicago, 1954.

Hotten, J. C., *The Slang Dictionary; or, The Vulgar Words, Street*

Phrases and "Fast" Expressions of High and Low Society, J. C. Hotten, London, 1865.

Huizinga, J. H., *Confessions of a European in England,* Heinemann, London, 1958.

Iversen, William, "A Short History of Swearing," *Playboy,* 8, September 1961, p. 101 *ff.*

Jespersen, Otto, *Language: Its Nature, Development and Origin,* Holt, New York, 1922.

Jespersen, Otto, *Mankind, Nation and Indiviual from a Linguistic Point of View,* Harvard U. Press, Cambridge, 1925.

Jespersen, Otto, "Veiled Language," Society for Pure English, Tract #33, Oxford, 1929, pp. 420-430.

Joesten, Joachim, "Calling Names in Any Language," *American Mercury,* 36, December 1935, pp. 483-487.

Joffe, Natalie F., "The Vernacular of Menstruation," *Word,* 4, December 1948, pp. 181-186.

Johnson, Burges, "Modern Maledictions, Execrations and Cusswords," *North American Review,* 238, November 1934, pp. 467-471.

Johnson, Burges, "The Every-day Profanity of Our Best People," *Century Magazine,* 92, June 1916, pp. 311-314.

Johnson, Burges, *The Lost Art of Profanity,* Bobbs-Merrill, Indianapolis and New York, 1948.

Johnson, Falk, "The History of Some 'Dirty' Words," *American Mercury,* 71, November 1950, pp. 538-545.

Jones, James, *From Here to Eternity,* Scribner's, New York, 1951.

Joyce, Patrick Weston, *English as We Speak It in Ireland*, Longmans, Green, London, 1910.

Junod, Henri Alexandre, *The Life of a South African Tribe*, 2nd ed., Macmillan, London, 1927.

Justinian, *Americana Sexualis,* privately printed, Chicago [1939].

Kilpatrick, James, *The Smut Peddlers*, Doubleday, Garden City, 1960.

Krassner, Paul, *Impolite Interviews*, Lyle Stuart, New York, 1961.

Kronhausen, Eberhard, and Kronhausen, Phyllis, *Pornography and the Law: The Psychology of Erotic Realism and Pornography*, Ballantine Books, New York, 1959.

La Barre, Weston, "Obscenity: An Anthropological Appraisal," *Law and Contemporary Problems,* 20, Autumn 1955, pp. 533-543.

Lawrence, D. H., *Pornography and Obscenity*, Knopf, New York, 1930.

Leem, Knud, "An Account of the Laplanders of Finmark," *in* Pinkerton, J., Vol. 1, *q.v.*

Legman, G., "The Bawdy Song . . . in Fact and in Print," *Explorations* (published by University of Toronto), 7, pp. 139-156.

Legman, G., *Misconceptions in the Collecting and Interpreting of Erotic Folklore,* unpublished, n.d.; typescript at Institute for Sex Research, Inc., Bloomington, Ind.

Loth, David, *The Erotic in Literature: A Historical Survey of Pornography as Delightful as It Is Indiscreet,* Messner, New York, 1961.

Lyall, Archibald, *It Isn't Done; or The Future of Taboo among the British Islanders,* K. Paul, Trench,. Trubner, London, 1930; revised edition, *The Future of Taboo in These Islands*, 1936.

Macdonell, A. A., "Vedic Religion," *in* Hastings, James, ed., *Encyclopaedia of Religion and Ethics,* Vol. 12, *q.v.*

MacDougald, Duncan, Jr., "Language and Sex," *in* Albert Ellis and Albert Abarbanel, eds., *The Encyclopedia of Sexual Behavior,* *q.v.*

MacKenzie, Duncan R., *The Spirit-Ridden Konde,* Seeley, Service, London, 1925.

Mailer, Norman, *The Naked and the Dead,* Rinehart, New York, 1948.

Malinowski, Bronislaw, *Sex and Repression in Savage Society,* Meridian Books, New York, 1955.

Mathews, Mitford M., ed., *A Dictionary of Americanisms on Historical Principles,* 2 vols., U. of Chicago Press, Chicago, 1951.

Maurer, David W., "Prostitutes and Criminal Argots," *American Journal of Sociology,* 44, January 1939, pp. 546-550.

Mayberry, George, *A Concise Dictionary of Abbreviations,* Tudor, New York, 1961; *see also* review in *Life,* 50, June 30, 1961, p. 19.

McAtee, W. L., *Nomina Abitera,* privately printed, 1945.

Mencken, H. L., *The American Language,* 4th ed., Knopf, New York, 1936.

Mencken, H. L., *Supplement I, The American Language,* Knopf, New York, 1945.

Meredith, Mamie, "Inexpressibles, Unmentionables, Unwhisperables, and Other Verbal Delicacies of the Mid-Nineteenth Century Americans," *American Speech,* 5, April 1930, pp. 285-287.

New Canting Dictionary Comprehending All the Terms, Ancient and Modern, Used in the Several Tribes of Gypsies, Beggars, etc., privately printed, London, 1725.

Newman, Stanley S., *see* Spier, Leslie, Hallowell, A. Irving, and Newman, Stanley S.

Nicholson, Margaret, *A Dictionary of American-English Usage Based on Fowler's Modern English Usage,* Oxford, New York, 1957.

Ogden, C. K., and Richards, I. A., *The Meaning of Meaning: A Study of the Influence of Language upon Thought and of the Science of Symbolism,* Harcourt, Brace, New York, 5th ed., 1938.

Packard, Frederick, "Schizoverbia," *New Yorker,* 21, Jan. 12, 1946, pp. 83-84.

Paget, Richard, *Human Speech,* Harcourt, Brace, New York, 1930.

Partridge, Eric, ed., *A Classical Dictionary of the Vulgar Tongue,* by Captain Grose, Scholartis Press, 1931.

Partridge, Eric, *A Dictionary of Slang and Unconventional English,* Macmillan, New York, 1938, and Routledge and Kegan Paul, London, 1949.

Partridge, Eric, *A Dictionary of the Underworld, British and American,* Macmillan, New York, 1950.

Partridge, Eric, *Origins: A Short Etymological Dictionary of Modern English,* Routledge and Kegan Paul, London, 1958.

Partridge, Eric, *Shakespeare's Bawdy: A Literary and Psychological Essay and a Comprehensive Glossary,* Routledge, London, 1947.

Partridge, Eric, *Slang To-day and Yesterday,* Macmillan, New York, 1934.

Partridge, Eric, *Words, Words, Words!* Methuen, London, 1933.

Pei, Mario, and Gaynor, Frank, *A Dictionary of Linguistics,* Philosophical Library, New York, 1954.

Pei, Mario, *The Story of Language*, Lippincott, Philadelphia and New York, 1949.

Pike, Kenneth L., *Language in Relation to a Unified Theory of the Structure of Human Behavior*, Summer Institute of Linguistics, Glendale, Calif., 1954.

Pinkerton, J., *A General Collection of the Best and Most Interesting Voyages and Travels in All Parts of the World*, 17 vols., Longman, Hurst, London, 1808-1814, Vol. 1.

Radcliffe-Brown, A. R., "Introduction to the Analysis of Kinship Systems," *in* Bell, Norman W., and Vogel, Ezra F., *A Modern Introduction to the Family, q.v.*

Randolph, Vance, *Bawdy Elements in the Ozark Speech*, unpublished, 1954; typescript at Institute for Sex Research, Inc., Bloomington, Ind.

Randolph, Vance, and Wilson, George P., *Down in the Holler: A Gallery of Ozark Folk Speech*, U. of Oklahoma Press, Norman, Okla., 1953.

Randolph, Vance, *Pissing in the Snow and Other Ozark Folktales*, unpublished, 1954; typescript at Institute for Sex Research, Inc. Bloomington, Ind.

Randolph, Vance, *"Unprintable" Songs from the Ozarks*, 2 vols., unpublished, 1954; typescript at Institute for Sex Research, Inc. Bloomington, Ind.

Randolph, Vance, "Verbal Modesty in the Ozarks," *Dialect Notes*, 6, 1928, pp. 37-64.

Randolph, Vance, *Vulgar Rhymes from the Ozarks*, unpublished, 1954; typescript at Institute for Sex Research, Inc. Bloomington, Ind.

Read, Allen Walker,"An Obscenity Symbol," *American Speech,* 9, December 1934, pp. 264-278.

Read, Allen Walker, *Lexical Evidence from Folk Epigraphy in Western North America: A Glossarial Study of the Low Element in the English Vocabulary,* privately printed, Paris, 1935.

Read, Allen Walker, "Noah Webster as a Euphemist," *Dialect Notes,* 6, 1934, pp. 385-391.

Richards, I. A., *see* Ogden, C. K., and Richards, I. A.

Riesman, David, with Glazer, Nathan, and Denney, Reuel, *The Lonely Crowd: A Study of the Changing American Character,* abridged by the authors, Doubleday, New York, 1953.

Roback, A. A., *A Dictionary of the International Slurs (Ethnophaulisms) with a Supplementary Essay on Aspects of Ethnic Prejudice,* Sci-Art Publishers, Cambridge, Mass., 1944.

Roth, Walter, *Ethnological Studies among the North-West-Central Queensland Aborigines,* London.

St. John-Stevas, Norman, *Obscenity and the Law,* Secker & Warburg, London, 1956.

Sallengre, Albert H., *Novus Thesaurus Antiquitatum Romanarum,* 3 vols., 1716-1719.

Sapir, Edward, *Culture, Language and Personality,* U. of California Press, Berkeley and Los Angeles, 1960.

Sapir, Edward, *Language: An Introduction to the Study of Speech,* Harcourt, Brace, New York, 1949.

Sapir, Edward, *Selected Writings in Language, Culture and Personality,* U. of California Press, Berkeley, 1951.

Saussure, Ferdinand de, *Course in General Linguistics,* Philosophical Library, New York, 1959.

Schlauch, Margaret, *The Gift of Tongues,* Modern Age, New York, 1942; republished under title *The Gift of Language,* Dover, New York, 1955.

Schmidt, J. E., *Libido,* Charles C Thomas, Springfield, Ill., 1960.

Schmidt, J. E., *Narcotics Lingo and Lore,* Charles C Thomas, Springfield, Ill., 1959.

Seagle, William, *see* Ernst, Morris L., and Seagle, William.

Sillitoe, Alan, *Saturday Night and Sunday Morning,* Knopf, New York, 1959.

Sperber, Hans, *see* Estrich, Robert M., and Sperber, Hans.

Spier, Leslie, Hallowell, A., and Norman, Stanley S., eds., *Language, Culture, and Personality: Essays in Memory of Edward Sapir,* Sapir Memorial Publication Fund, Menasha, Wisc., 1941.

Steadman, John Marcellus, "A Study of Verbal Taboos," *American Speech,* 10, April 1935, pp. 93-103.

Tallent-Bateman, Charles T., "The Etymology of Some Common Exclamations," *Manchester Literary Club Papers,* 12, 1886, pp. 345-356.

Taylor, Anna M., *The Language of World War II,* H. W. Wilson, New York, 1944; revised edition, 1948.

Thornton, Henry, and Thornton, Freda, *How to Achieve Sex Happiness in Marriage,* Vanguard Press, New York, 1939.

Twain, Mark, *Conversation as It Was by the Social Fireside in the Time of the Tudors (1601),* Lyle Stuart, New York [1962].

United States Fleet, United States Naval Forces, Germany, *Swear Words, Oaths, and Terms of Vulgarity Used in the U.S.S.R.*, mimeographed, n.d., stamped "Restricted" and "Obscene."

Valdes, Edgar, "The Art of Swearing," *Belgravia,* 88, December 1895, pp. 366-379.

Van den Bark, Melvin, *see* Berrey, Lester V., and Van den Bark, Melvin.

Vogel, Ezra F., *see* Bell, Norman W., and Vogel, Ezra F.

Wain, John, *Living in the Present,* Secker & Warburg, London, 1955.

Wallace, Alfred R., "The Expressiveness of Speech, or Mouth-Gesture as a Factor in the Origin of Language,"*Fortnightly Review,* 64, (n.s. 58), 1895, pp. 528-543.

Weber, Carl Jefferson, *English-American Dictionary,* unpublished, 1917; through the courtesy of Allen Walker Read.

Webster's Third New International Dictionary of the English Language, Merriam Co., Springfield, Mass., 1961.

Weingarten, Joseph A., *An American Dictionary of Slang and Colloquial Speech,* published by the author, New York, 1954.

Wentworth, Harold, and Flexner, Stuart Berg, *Dictionary of American Slang,* Thomas Y. Crowell, New York, 1960.

Wentworth, Harold, "'Sandwich' Words and Rime-Caused Nonce Words," *Philological Studies, West Virginia U. Bulletin,* 40(3), September 1939, pp. 65-71.

Weseen, Maurice, *Dictionary of American Slang,* Thomas Y. Crowell, New York, 1934.

Whitman, Walt, *An American Primer,* Small, Maynard & Co., Boston, 1904.

Whorf, Benjamin Lee, *Language, Thought, and Reality,* Technology Press of M.I.T. and John Wiley, New York, 1959.

Whorf, Benjamin Lee, "The Relation of Habitual Thought and Behavior to Language," reprinted in Spier, Leslie, ed., *Language, Culture, and Personality; Essays in Memory of Edward Sapir, q.v.,* and in *Language, Thought, and Reality, supra.*

Wilcox, Claire, ed., *Civil Liberties under Attack,* U. of Pennsylvania Press, Philadelphia, 1951.

Wilson, George P., *see* Randolph, Vance, and Wilson, George P.

Woolf, H. B., *The G. I.'s Favorite Four-Letter Word,* privately printed [Baton Rouge, La., 1948].

Wylie, Philip, *Opus 21,* Rinehart, New York, 1949.

GENERAL INDEX

Abarbanel, A., *see* Ellis, A., and Abarbanel, A.

Affirmative qualities of tabooed words, 56-7, 77-8, 90-1

Alcott, Amos B., 101

Alcott, Louisa May, 101

Alcox, Amos B., 101

Alcox, Louisa May, 101

Ambiguities, 163-4

Ambivalent attitude toward sex, 123-5

Anglo-Saxonisms, 47

Animism and taboo, 27-8

Army slang, 57, 141

Barrère, A., 57n.

Bell, N. W., and Vogel, E. F., 22n.

Berrey, L. V., and Van den Bark, M., 52, 55, 57, 77n., 110, 130n.

Blacklists and excretion, 55

Blasphemy, 40, 66-7

Bloomfield, L., 28, 35n., 100

Boal, S., 147n.

Bonwit Teller, 85

Breasts, synonyms for, 123-5

Briffault, R., 21n.

Buck, C. D., 138

Burke, W. J., 39n., 41n., 114

Buttocks, terminology for, 85

Cacophemisms, 15, 115-6, 118

Cant, 37-8

Carnoy, A., 115

Cary, H. N., 110, 138

Chesterton, G. K., 31*n.*
Children, attitudes of, 101
Class differences and slang, 34-5
Clemens, S. L., *see* Twain, Mark
Coates, F., 147
Cockney English, 147
Comstock, A., 70, 172
Condom, synonyms for, 155
Cory, D. W., 111, 112
Courage and slang, 91
Crane, S., 167
Creolization, 97
Criminal slang, 63

Defecation, slang for, 50-60
Denney, R., see Riesman, D., *et al.*
Deviant cases, *see* Affirmative qualities of tabooed words
De Voto, B., 168
Dirty words, as a generic term, 41
Dysphemisms, 115-6. *See also* Cacophemisms

Ejaculation, 154-8
Elliot, A. G., 132
Ellis, A., 14, 15, 16, 41*n.*, 123, 143, 169, 173
Ellis, A., and Abarbanel, A., 84*n.*
Ellis, H., 164
Emission, nocturnal, 119-20
England, slang in, 94, 100, 131-2
Epictetus, 162
Epithets, 106-12
Erotic desire and slang, 95, 96
Eskimos, 21
Estrich, R. M., and Sperber, H., 165*n.*

Ethnic slurs, 38-40
Ethnophaulisms, 38-40
Etymologies, 47, 51, 61-2, 138
Euphemisms, 61-2, 70, 74, 114-20, 127
Evans-Pritchard, E. E., 24-5
Evasions, linguistic, 163-4. *See also* Euphemisms
Excretion, slang for, 50-78
Expletives, 53, 88, 139

Farmer, J. S., 56, 139, 142
Fellation and slang, 109-12
Fitch, R. E., 168-9
Flexner, S. B., *see* Wentworth, H., and Flexner, S. B.
Folklore, reports of, 165
Foreign words and slang, 98
Foreign words as euphemisms, 69-70
Four-letter words, 47
Fowler, H. W., 151
Franklyn, J., 147
Frazer, J., 27, 28*n.*
French euphemisms, 70
French slang, 57, 100
Fright and defecation, 63-4
From Here to Eternity, 166-8, 169

Gaynor, F., *see* Pei, M., and Gaynor, F.
Glazer, N., *see* Reisman, D., *et al.*
Goldin, H. E., 38*n.*
Grammar and slang, 36*ff.*
Graves, R., 68, 85, 164
Grose, Capt., 53*n.*, 56

Haney, R. W., 166
Hanneken, P. L., 24
Harper, R. A., 111
Hastings, J., 24*n.*
Hayden, M. G., 107*n.*
Henley, W. E., *see* Farmer, J. S.
Hills, E. C., 41*n.*
Hoijer, H., 174*n.*
Homonyms, 100, 137-8
Homosexuality, 111-2
Hopper, R., 14
Horton, J. P., 149*n.*
Hotten, J. C., 33*n.*
Huizinga, J. H., 60*n.*
Humiliation and excretion, 54

Illegitimacy and slang, 108-9
Incest, fear of, 139
Infixes, 146-8
Infrahumans and slang, 96-7
Inge, W. R., 142
Initials, 51-2, 54, 55, 57, 62, 69
Insanity, slang for, 88-90
Institute for Sex Research, 14, 24*n.*, 96*n.*, 110*n.*
Involuntary emission, 119-20
Iversen, W., 45*n.*, 47*n.*

Jargon, 37-8
Jespersen, O., 46
Jewish slang, 98
Joffe, N. F., 119
Johnson, B., 31*n.*, 164*n.*, 165
Jones, J., 166-8, 169
Joyce, J., 166, 172
Junod, H. A., 24
Justinian, 97

k, as phoneme, 84
Kinsey, A. C., 14
Kinship and language, 21-2
Kipling, R., 167
Krassner, P., 41*n.*, 143*n.*

La Barre, W., 165
Language and culture, 18*ff.*
Lawrence, D. H., 116, 172
Leem, K., 24
Legitimate meanings of tabooed words, 99-101
Legman, G., 165
Life, 54*n.*, 167-8
Little Men, 101
Little Women, 101
Luck, slang expressions for, 94-6

Macdonell, A. A., 24
MacDougald, D., 84
MacKenzie, D., 24
Mailer, N., 47*n.*, 166
Malinowski, B., 119-20
Marines, 77
Masculinity and slang, 92
Masturbation, 114-7, 118
Mathews, M. M., 56, 130*n.*
McAtee, W. L., 56*n.*
Mencken, H. L., 39*n.*, 41*n.*, 70, 73, 85, 90, 101, 147, 149
Mendacity and slang, 54, 58
Menstruation, 118
Merriam Webster dictionary, 51*n.*, 52, 166, 167
Miller, H., 172
Modified swearing, 67-8
Montagu, A., 146-7, 148, 149

Naked and the Dead, 142
Names, proscribed, 27
Navy slang, 55, 72, 141
Nerve, slang expressions for, 95-6
New Canting Dictionary, 97n.
New York Post, 147n.
New York Times, 67, 68, 85, 137n., 166
Nicholson, M., 151n.
Nocturnal emission, 119-20

Obscenity in primitive societies, 22-5
Old Testament, 28-9
Onomatopoeia, 51
Organs of excretion and sexuality, 80-104
Origins of tabooed words, *see* Etymologies
Ostentation, slang for, 95-6
Oxford English Dictionary, 78
Ozarks, 74, 96, 100, 101, 127

Packard, F., 150-1
Paget, R., 51, 84
Partridge, E., 33n., 52-3, 138
Peer groups, 122
Pei, M., 74, 166
Pei, M., and Gaynor, F., 151
Pejoratives, 106-12
  ethnic, 38-40
Penis, personification of, 102-4
  slang for, 93-8
  synonyms for, 82ff.
Physiology and slang, 80-104
Pinkerton, J., 24n.
Platt, G., 14

Pollution, as culturally-defined phenomenon, 120
Poolroom slang, 94-5
Pope, A., 169
Porter, K. A., 10-1
Primitive groups, taboo among, 26-9
Profanity, meaning of term, 126
Pulitzer, J., 147
Puritanism, and homosexuality, 111
  and taboo, 172-4

r, inserted into tabooed words, 90
Radcliffe-Brown, A. R., 22
Randolph, V., 96, 101
Randolph, V., and Wilson, G. P., 74, 78n., 100, 127
Read, A. W., 9-12, 14, 15, 16, 24, 41n., 44, 47n., 115, 132n.
Rectum, slang for, 93-8
Reprobate, expressions for, 55
Riesman, D., *et al.,* 57, 125n., 137n.
Rituals and obscenity, 24-5
Roback, A. A., 39
Role differentiation and slang, 34-5
Roth, W., 24

Sagarin, A. B., 77n.
Sallengre, A. H., 24n.
Sandwich words, 148-9
Sapir, E., 13, 19, 20, 21, 42, 148, 174
Sapir-Whorf hypothesis, 14, 16
Schizophrasia, 151-2
Schizoverbia, 150-1
Schlauch, M., 35n.

Segura, G., 91*n.*
Semen, language for, 154-8
Sex, euphemisms for, 46-7, 127-8
  official language of, 46-7
  slang of, 41
  tabooed words for, 47-9, 127*ff.*
Sheer, B., 170*n.*
Sillitoe, A., 147
Sin, in language, 21
Slang, origin and function, 33*ff.*
  sources of, 161
Smollett, T., 164
Spanish slang, 91
Sperber, H., *see* Estrich, R. M., and Sperber, H.
Spier, L., 174*n.*
Suffixes, 97
Surnames, 87

Tabooed words, 22*ff.*
  in primitive societies, 26*ff.*
  relaxation of, 163*ff.*
Ten Commandments, 28-9
Testicles, terminology for, 84, 86-92
Thornton, H. and F., 41*n.*
Tmesis, 151
Toilet, synonyms for, 69-74
Tolstoy, L., 167
Twain, Mark, 168

Ulysses, 166
Untenability, expressed in slang, 54-5
Urination, slang for, 61-4

Van den Bark, M., *see* Berrey, L V., and Van den Bark, M.
Vassar, 73
Virgin, language for, 21
Vogel, E. F., *see* Bell, N. W., and Vogel, E. F.

Wain, J., 147
Wallace, A. R., 83
Weber, C. J., 132
Webster, *see* Merriam Webster dictionary
Wentworth, H., 148, 149
Wentworth, H., and Flexner, S. B., 41*n.*, 56, 107*n.*, 130*n.*, 155
Weseen, M., 38*n.*, 149
Whitman, W., 42, 164
Whorf, B. L., 13, 20, 174
Wilson, G. P., *see* Randolph, V., and Wilson, G. P.
Woolsey, Judge, 166
Word fetishism, 9
Wylie, P., 170-1

Yiddish slang, 98

INDEX OF WORDS AND PHRASES

about a dog, see a man, 71
absobleedinglutely, 147
abso-bloody-lutely, 147
abuse, self-, 116
ace in the hole, 37
affair, have an, 127-8
agreeable, disinfuck-, 148
ain't, 37
Alcox, 101
all-bleedin'-mighty, 147
all fouled up, situation normal, 141
all fucked up, situation normal, 141
all screwed up, 135
all, you-, 37
Anglo-Saxon monosyllable, 138

apples, 134
applesauce, 161
around, fuck, 110, 140
around, jerking, 117
around, sleep, 127
ass, 42, 85, 95, 98, 100, 106
ass, an, 93, 94
ass, big 96
asses, fat, 85
ass, for kiss my, 40
ass, he's got, 94
ass, horse's, 96
ass, perfect, 96, 97
ass, piece of, 95
ass, plenty of, 94
ass, shit-, 55
ass, silly, 96, 97

ass, stubborn, 96
ass, takes a lot of, 95
assy, 95
assy catch, 95
assy, is he, 95
away, piss, 62, 63

baby, shut the —— up, 152
baby, sit the —— down, 152
backside, 85
bacon, 161
bad, just too damn, 53
bags, 124
Ball, 87
ball, 86
ball, carries the, 87
ball of fire, 88, 161
ball of his foot, 87
ball, on the, 87
balloons, 123
Balls, 87
balls, 42, 48, 84, 86, 87, 88, 90,
    98, 123, 129, 139
balls, carrying the, 88
ball, screw-, 132
balls, he's got, 91, 94
balls of his feet, 87
balls, oh, 88
balls, on the, 88
balls, you have, 92
bastard, 107, 108, 109, 111
bastard, son-of-a-bitch, 109
bathroom, 47, 71, 73
bats, 89
batty, 89
beans, great jumping, 68
bed, 100
bed, go to, 46, 100

bee, son-of-a-, 107
beeyem, 52
behind, 85
being nutty, 89
big ass, 96
big prick, 97, 102-4, 135
biscuit, son-of-a-, 107
bitch, 107, 108
bitch bastard, son-of-a-, 109
bitch, son-of-a-, 107, 108
bleeding, 147
bleedinglutely, abso-, 147
bleedin'-mighty, all-, 147
bloody, 142, 146, 147, 148
bloody-lutely, abso-, 147
bloody-possible, im-, 147
bloody side, out, 147
bloodywell, 147
B. M., 52
B. M., to make, 52
bologna, 161
boobs, 124
born out of wedlock, 108
bosom, 123
bowel movement, have a, 48, 52
bowel movement, having a, 46
bowels, moving the, 46
boy's room, little, 71
bread, 37, 161
bread and water, 63
bull tales, cock and, 101
bum, 94
bumps, 123
bush, 124
buttocks, 72
buzzard shit, 57

came, 155

can, 72, 85
can, going to the, 73
can it, 72
canned, got, 72
cap, feather in the, 161
care a hoot, don't, 143
carries the ball, 87
carrying the balls, 88
catch, an assy, 95
caught with his pants down, 64
cherry, 124
chier, 51, 57
chier du poivre, 57
chier, vous me faites, 57
child of love, 108
choke, 161
Christ, 28, 40
Christ's sake, for, 40, 107
climax, 154
cloak room, 71
cock, 42, 48, 84, 100, 101, 109
cock-a-doodle-doo, 101
cock a gun, 101
cock and bull tales, 101
cock, hay-, 100
cockroach, 101
C-sucker, 110
c—— ——r, 111
cocksucker, 109-11
cock, weather-, 101
cohabit, 128
cohabitation, 45, 46, 82
cojonudo es, que, 91
cold as hell, 41
come, 48, 154
comfort station, public, 70
coney, 100
connil, 100
connin, 100

conscious, unfuckin-, 148
copulate, 48, 128
copulation, 45, 46, 82
corruption, shit, piss and, 64-5
coxswain, 101
cracker, 40
crap, 57, 58, 76, 171
crap, full of, 58
crap, take a, 57
crap, that's, 58
crap, what's all this, 58
crazy as a shitepoke, 56
creek, up shit, 54
creek, up shit's, 55
creek, up shit's —— without a paddle, 55
Cripes, 40, 66
crud, 155
crying out loud, for, 40, 66, 107
cunt, 84, 166, 167, 168
curd, 155
cuss words, 41
cut no ice, 161
cutter, piss-, 77

damn, 28, 40
damn, don't give a, 143
damn, tinker's, 143
dam, tinker's, 143
darn, 40, 66
defecate, 48
defecation, 45
derrière, 85
derrières, large, 85
detumescence, 45, 48
devil, 28
dick, 42, 48, 84
disafuckingreeable, 148

disagreeable, fuckin, 148
disinfuckagreeable, 148
dog, fuck the, 140
dog, see a man about a, 71
do his duty, 61
do it, 46
donkey, 100
don't care a hoot, 143
don't give a damn, 143
don't give a fuck, 143
don't give a shit, 56, 143
don't, he, 37
dough, 37, 161
do your duty, 47
dream, wet, 119
duty, do his, 61
duty, do your, 47

ears, prick-, 97
ecstasy, nocturnal, 120
ejaculate, 48
ejaculation, 45
emission, nocturnal, 119
erection, 45, 48

F, 171
f, 137
face, prick-, 97
facts of life, 163
facts of sex, 163
fantasy, nocturnal, 120
fat asses, 85
feather in the cap, 161
feces, 45, 48
feet, balls of his, 87
fellator, 109
fellatrix, 109
ferk, 90

fike, 138
fire, ball of, 88, 161
fix his wagon, 37
flat, go, 48
foot, ball of his, 87
for Christ's sake, 40, 107
for crying out loud, 40, 66, 107
for kiss my ass, 40
fornicate, 46
fornication, 45
fouled up, 140
fouled up, situation normal all,
    141
four-letter word, 47, 137
Fred, 73
f——, 137
f***, 137
fuck, 42, 48, 128, 137, 139, 143,
    144, 166, 167, 168
fuckagreeable, disin-, 148
fuck around, 110, 140
fuck, don't give a, 143
fucked, got, 140
fucked up, 140
fucked up, situation normal all,
    141
fucken, 142
fuckenganda, propa-, 149
fucker, 139
Fucker, John le, 138
fucker, mother-, 139
fuckin, 142, 143, 148, 152
fuckin', 142
fuckinconscious, un-, 148
fuckin four, half past, 152
fucking, 142
fucking, got a, 140
fuckin good friend, 142, 143
fuckingreeable, disa-, 148

fuckinpossible, im-, 148
fuckinsponsible, irre-, 148
fuck, oh, 140
fuck, shut the —— up, 152
fuck, sit the —— down, 152
fuck, the, 151, 152
fuck the dog, 140
fuck you, 143
fuck yourself, go, 57, 143
fuck your way out of a situation, 140
fudge, 68
fudge, oh, 140
full of crap, 58
full of piss and vinegar, 78
full of shit, 54, 76
fyke, 138

gee whiz, 41
gee ziz, 41
get laid, 128
get screwed, 134
girl's room, little, 71
give a damn, don't, 143
give a fuck, don't, 143
give a shit, don't, 56, 143
God, 28, 29, 40, 90
goddam, 148
goddam, inde——pendent, 147
goddammit, 40
goddamnation, obli-, 147
God, oh my, 41
go flat, 48
go fuck yourself, 57, 143
going to the can, 73
going to the head, 72
goldarnit, 40
go limp, 48

gone nuts, 89
good, fuckin, 142, 143
goose, 161
go screw yourself, 130
gosh, 40, 66, 90
got a fucking, 140
got a screwing, 134, 140
got ass, he's, 94
got balls, he's, 91, 94
got canned, 72
got fucked, 140
got guts, he's, 91
got my revenge, 155
go to bed, 100
go to bed with, 46
go to hell, 126
got screwed, 140
go unfuck yourself, 143
grapefruits, 124
gravy, 37
great jumping beans, 68
green, shitting, 64
growths, 124
gun, son-of-a-, 107
guts, he's got, 91

half past fuckin four, 152
hard-on, 48
have a bowel movement, 48, 52
have an affair, 127-8
have balls, you, 92
have nuts, you, 91
have sex, 46
have sexual intercourse, 46, 128
having a bowel movement, 46
haycock, 100
haystack, 101
head, 72

head, going to the, 72
headlights, 123
heaven, 28
heck, 41
he don't, 37
heel, shit-, 55
hell, 28, 40, 41
hell, cold as, 41
hell, go to, 126
hell, hot as, 40
hell, oh, 40
hell, to —— with it, 40
herself, play with, 115
he's got ass, 94
he's got balls, 91, 94
he's got guts, 91
himself, play by, 115
himself, play with, 115
hole, ace in the, 37
holy shit, 55
honey, 161
hoot, don't care a, 143
horse's ass, 96
hot as hell, 40
house, in the shit-, 76
house, nut, 89
house, out-, 71
house, shit-, 71, 76
huevos, 91
huevudo es, que, 91
hush money, 37

ice, cut no, 161
im-bloody-possible, 147
imfuckinpossible, 148
impossible, fuckin, 148
indegoddampendent, 147
intercourse, have sexual, 46

in the shithouse, 76
irrefuckinsponsible, 148
irresponsible, fuckin, 148
is he assy, 95
it, can ——, 72

jack off, 116
jay, 73
jerk, 117
jerking around, 117
jerk off, 116
Jesus, 28, 40, 41
Jesus, jumping, 126
John, 73, 74
john, 73
johnnie, 73
jouir, 154
jumping beans, great, 68
jumping Jesus, 126
just too damn bad, 53

kiss my ass, 40
knobs, 123
knocked up, 100
knock the shit out of, 54

ladies' room, 71
laid, 129
laid, get, 128
large *derrières,* 85
lay, 128, 129
lay down, 100
leave the room, 72
lemons, 124
life, facts of, 163
limp, go, 48

list, shit-, 55
little boy's room, 71
little girl's room, 71
little thing, your, 83
looking up, 140
loony, 89
loose, a screw, 132
lot of ass, it takes a, 95
loud, for crying out, 40, 66, 107
love, 127
love, to make, 46, 127
luck, shit out of, 55, 110
luck, tough, 53, 54
lungs, 123

make B. M., 52
make love, 46, 127
make me shit, you, 57
make shit out of, 54
make, to ——, 47, 87
make water, 47
make weewee, 47, 61
man about a dog, see a, 71
masturbation, 115, 117
melons, 124
men's room, 71
merde, 53, 169, 171
micturition, 45
milk bottles, 124
milkers, 124
molehills, 123
money, hush, 37
mosob, 123
mother-fucker, 139
movement, have a bowel, 46, 48, 52
moving the bowels, 46
my God, oh, 41

nerts, 90
nincompoop, 91
nocturnal ecstasy, 120
nocturnal emission, 119
nocturnal fantasy, 120
nocturnal pollution, 119, 120
nocturnal tension relief, 120
normal all fouled up, situation, 141
normal all screwed up, situation, 141
nut, a, 89
nut house, 89
nuts, 48, 88, 89, 90, 123, 131, 171
nuts, gone, 89
nuts, oh, 88
nuts, you have, 91
nuts, you're, 88
nutty, 88

obligodamnation, 147
off, 117
off, jack ——, 116
off, jerk ——, 116
off, pissed ——, 62, 76
off, pull ——, 116
oh balls, 88
oh fuck, 140
oh fudge, 140
oh hell, 40
oh my, 41
oh my God, 41
oh nuts, 88
oh shit, 53
onanism, 115
on the ball, 87
on the balls, 88
oranges, 124

ordinary prick, 97
organ, 47, 82, 83
oui, oui, 62
out bloody side, 147
outhouse, 71, 87
out-of-luck, shit-, 110
out-of-wedlock, 111
out, put ——, 62
ox stories, rooster and, 101

P, 52, 128
paddle, up shit's creek without a, 55
panther piss, 63
pants down, caught with his, 64
pants, shitting in his, 64
pause that refreshes, 78
pea, 42, 51, 52, 128
pee, 51, 52
peepee, 52
pellets, 123
pendejo, 91, 106
penis, 45, 48, 82, 83, 84
perfect ass, 96, 97
perfect prick, 102-4
Peter, 74
phoque, 137
piece of ass, 95
pig, be a, 161
pipe, 124
piss, 42, 48, 51, 52, 62, 83, 98, 129
piss and corruption, shit ——, 64-5
piss and punk, 63
piss and vinegar, full of, 78
piss away, 62, 63
piss-cutter, 77
pissed off, 62, 76

pisse, pisse, 62
pisser, 77, 91
pisser (Fr.), 51
pisshouse, 63
pissoir, 51
piss, panther, 63
pisspiration, 63
pisspire, 63
piss through the same quill, 78
piss-whiz, 77
plates, 124
play by himself, 115
play with himself, 115
plenty of ass, 94
P.O.'ed, 54, 62
pollution, nocturnal, 119, 120
possible, im-bloody-, 147
potty, sitting on the, 45
powder room, 71
prick, 42, 48, 84, 97, 98, 99
prick, a, 94
prick, big, 97, 102-4, 135
prick-ears, 97
prick-face, 97
prickicity, 94, 97
prickiness, 94
prick, ordinary, 97
prick, perfect, 102-4
prick, silly, 97
privates, 47, 81, 82
propafuckenganda, 149
propaganda, fuckin, 149
public comfort station, 70
pull off, 116
pumps, 124
pump shit, 59, 60
punk, piss and, 63
pussy, 84

put out, 62
put the screws on, 130, 131

que cojonudo es, 91
que huevudo es, 91
quill, piss through the same, 78

racks, 124
ragamuffins, 151
ragged little muffins, 151
refreshes, pause that, 78
relations, have sexual, 128
rest room, 71
retire, 100
retiring-room, 70
revenge, got my, 155
rigamarole, 151
rigged-up marole, 151
roach, 101
room, bath-, 73
room, cloak, 71
room, ladies', 71
room, leave the, 72
room, little boy's, 71
room, little girl's, 71
room, men's, 71
room, powder, 71
room, rest, 71
room, wash-, 71
rooster, 100
rooster and ox stories, 101
roosters, pull back both, 101
roosterswain, 101
royal screwing, 134

sack, sh-t, 56
sake, for Christ's, 40, 107

scared shitless, 64
screw, 42, 48, 128, 129, 130, 131, 132, 133, 135
screw, a, 130
screwball, 132
screwed, get, 134
screwed, got, 140
screwed up, 133, 134, 135, 140
screwed up, all, 135
screwing, got a, 134, 140
screwing, royal, 134
screw loose, 132
screws on, put the, 130, 131
screwy, 130, 131
screw yourself, go, 130
scrotum, 45, 48, 82, 83
scum, 155, 156, 157
scum bag, 155
scum of the earth, 156
see a man about a dog, 71
self-abuse, 116
semen, 45, 155
sex, have, 46
sexual intercourse, have, 46
sexual relations, have, 128
sheet, 68
shert, 90
shingles, shit on, 57
s**t, 129
shit, 42, 48, 51, 52, 53, 54, 55, 56, 57, 67, 68, 76, 77, 90, 98, 117, 129, 139, 140, 166, 167, 168, 169, 171
shit a smoke, 56
shit-ass, 55
shit, buzzard, 57
shit creek, up, 54
shit, don't give a, 56, 143
shitepoke, 56

shitepoke, crazy as a, 56
shit, full of, 54, 76
shit-heel, 55
shit, holy, 55
shithouse, 71, 76
shithouse, in the, 76
shit, knock the —— out of, 54
shitless, scared, 64
shit-list, 55
shit on shingles, 57
shit out of luck, 55, 110
shit, piss and corruption, 64-5
shit, pump, 59,60
sh-t sack, 56
shit's creek, up, 55
shit's creek, up —— without a paddle, 55
shit, take a, 48, 56
shitting green, 64
shitting in his pants, 64
shit, to make —— out of, 54
shit, tough, 53, 54, 62
shitty, 55
shit, you make me, 57
shit, what's all this, 58
shmuck, 98, 106
shoat, 55
shoot, 68
shoot, to, 48, 154, 155
short of luck, 55
shote, 55
shucks, 67, 68, 90, 101
shut the baby up, 152
shut the fuck up, 152
shut up, 72
shyte, 68
silly ass, 96, 97
silly prick, 97
sin, 21

sin, solitary, 116
sit the baby down, 152
sit the fuck down, 152
sitting on the potty, 45
situation, fuck your way out of a,
  140
situation normal all fouled up,
  141
situation normal all fucked up,
  141
sledding, tough, 54, 62
sleep, 127
sleep around, 46, 127
sleep with, 46, 127
sleeve, something up his, 37
slouch, be a, 161
smoke, shit a, 56
snafu, 54, 141
snafud, 141
snake, 40
s.o.b., 107
sociable, unfuckin-, 148
S.O.L., 54, 55
solitary sin, 116, 118
son-of-a-bee, 107
son-of-a-biscuit, 107
son-of-a-bitch, 107, 108
son-of-a-bitch bastard, 109
son-of-a-gun, 107
S.O.S., 57
station, public comfort, 70
stoolpigeon, 161
stubborn ass, 96
sugar, 67, 68, 90, 101, 140
sure out of luck, 55

take a crap, 57
take a shit, 48, 56
takes a lot of ass, 95

teats, 123
tension relief, nocturnal, 120
testicles, 45, 48, 82, 83, 87
that's crap, 58
thee, 37
the fuck, 151, 152
thing, your, 83
thing, your little, 83
thou, 37
tinker's dam, 143
tinker's damn, 143
tits, 123
TNT, 123
to hell with it, 40
toilet, 47, 70, 71, 72, 73
to let, 70
to make, 83
tonsils, 124
too damn bad, just, 53
tough luck, 53, 54
tough shit, 53, 54, 62
tough sledding, 54, 62
to usward, 151
T.S., 54, 62
tumescence, 45, 48
tu m' fais chier, 57
two nifty teats, 123

unconscious, fuckin, 148
unfuckinconscious, 148
unfuckinsociable, 148
unfuck yourself, go, 143
unsociable, fuckin, 148
up, fouled, 140
up, fucked, 140
up, looking, 140
up, screwed, 133, 134, 135, 140
up shit creek, 54

up shit's creek, 55
up shit's creek without a paddle,
    55
up, situation normal all fouled,
    141
up, situation normal all fucked,
    141
urethra, 45
urinate, 83
urination, 45, 48

vagina, 45
vinegar, full of piss and, 78
virgin, 21
vous me faites chier, 57

W, 70
wagon, fix his, 37
warts, 124
washroom, 70, 71
water, bread and, 63
water closet, 69
watermelons, 124
water, to make, 47
way out of a situation, fuck your,
    140
WC, 69
weathercock, 101
weathervane, 101
wedlock, born out of, 108
wedlock, out-of-, 111
weewee, 61, 62
weewee, to make, 47, 61
weewee, your, 83
well, for Christ's sake, 40
well, for kiss my ass, 40
wet dream, 119
what's all this crap, 58

what's all this shit, 58
what things soever, 151
whiz, piss-, 77
without a paddle, up shit's creek,
    55

you, 37
you-all, 37
you, fuck ——, 143
you have balls, 92

you have nuts, 91
you make me shit, 57
you're nuts, 88
your little thing, 83
yourself, go fuck, 143
yourself, go unfuck, 143
your thing, 83
your weewee, 83
yous, 37
youse, 37